GEORGE GERSHWIN
American Composer

Masters of Music

GEORGE GERSHWIN
American Composer

Catherine Reef

MORGAN
REYNOLDS
Incorporated

Greensboro

GEORGE GERSHWIN: AMERICAN COMPOSER

Photo Credits: Library of Congress

Library of Congress Cataloging-in-Publication Data

Reef, Catherine.
    George Gershwin : American Composer / Catherine Reef.
        p. cm. -- (Masters of music)
    Includes bibliographical references (p.) and index.
    Summary: Traces the life of the American Jewish composer who created a new kind of
music that has lasted beyond the fashion of his time.
    ISBN 1-883846-58-7 (hardcover)
        1. Gershwin, George, 1898-1937--Juvenile literature. 2. Composers--United
States--Biography--Juvenile literarure. [1. Gershwin, George, 1898-1937. 2. Composers.]
    I. Title. II. Masters of music (Greensboro, N.C.)

ML3930.G29 R44 2000
780'.92--dc21
[B]

                                                                        99-054031

Printed in the United States of America
First Edition

For the musicians in my family, past and present:
Walter H. Preston, Sr., and John S. Reef

Contents

Chapter One
This Modern Stuff 9

Chapter Two
Lucky Break 22

Chapter Three
A Kaleidoscope of America 32

Chapter Four
Composer? American? 44

Chapter Five
Carefree 56

Chapter Six
Music in Many Voices 66

Chapter Seven
Spirituals and Folk Songs 77

Chapter Eight
Final Years 91

Major Works 102
Glossary 103
Bibliography 104
Sources 106
Index 110

George Gershwin

Chapter One

This Modern Stuff

On a late summer day in 1910 a crowd gathered outside an apartment building on Second Avenue in New York City to watch a piano being hoisted into the air. Women in long, dark skirts and white shirtwaists and bearded men in black hats stretched their heads back. Their eyes tracked the heavy instrument as it inched higher and higher up the side of the building.

The piano was being delivered to the Gershvin apartment. Rose and Morris Gershvin had purchased the piano so their oldest son, Izzy, could learn to play. The Gershvins were Jewish immigrants from Russia and, like many of their neighbors, wanted to follow the customs of their adopted land. One of those customs, in the days before radio and inexpensive phonographs, was for middle-class Americans to have a piano in the parlor.

There also needed to be someone in the family who could play it. That's why fourteen-year-old Izzy fretted as he watched the workers guide the piano through a large window and set it down in the front room. He had no musical talent. He liked to spend his time reading and writing funny verses, not practicing scales and finger exercises.

As the piano was being delivered Izzy's brother George sauntered into the room. He smelled of sweat and rough play, and his hands and face were streaked with dirt. George Gershvin, nearly twelve, was the champion roller skater over on Seventh Street. He was as different from Izzy as a brother could be. He often skipped school and rarely did his homework, and his father worried that he would amount to nothing.

George gave the piano stool a spin or two, sat down, and raised the cover from the keyboard. Then, as his astonished family looked on, he played a polished version of a popular song. "I remember being particularly impressed by his swinging left hand," Izzy said later. The family agreed that George played just as well as the performers at the local vaudeville theater.

The Gershvins questioned George. How—and when—did he learn to play so skillfully? George shrugged and said it was no big deal. He had been fooling around on a player piano at a friend's house. Rose Gershvin announced then and there that George, and not Izzy, would be the one to take music lessons.

Music had first drawn George's attention when he was six years old. He stood outside a penny arcade listening to a mechanical piano play *Melody in F* by the composer and pianist Anton Rubinstein. "The peculiar jumps in the

George played piano professionally when he was a teenager.

music held me rooted," he recalled. For the rest of his life, whenever he heard Rubinstein's music, he pictured himself in front of the arcade, "standing there barefoot and in overalls, drinking it all in avidly."

At age ten, George sneaked out of an assembly at school. While most of the children at P.S. (Public School) 25 filed into the auditorium to hear eight-year-old Maxie Rosenzweig play the violin, George and his friends chose teams for a ball game. But when the strains of music reached the boys in the schoolyard, George forgot about baseball. He stood still, listening to the music. He had a "flashing revelation of beauty," he said. Even when it started to rain, he stayed where he was.

He presented himself, still wet, at the Rosenzweig apartment after school and asked to meet the young musician. Maxie was not at home. But his parents were so amused at George's appearance that they arranged for the boys to meet. George and Maxie quickly became close friends.

Maxie answered George's questions about music, and in turn, George introduced his new friend to some of his own interests, such as wrestling. He talked Maxie into playing hooky to savor the banquet of sights and sounds, aromas and flavors that was the Lower East Side of New York.

George's father, Morris Gershvin, born Moishe Gershovitz, had started out working in a shoe factory in the Russian city of St. Petersburg. In 1892 or 1893, he

Morris and Rose Gershvin immigrated to the United States from Russia at the end of the nineteenth century.

followed his girlfriend, Rose Bruskin, and her family to the Lower East Side. In New York he found a job as a foreman in a shoe factory and married Rose in 1895. The couple moved into an apartment over a pawnshop, and their first child, Israel, was born in 1896.

After arriving in the United States, Moishe Gershovitz changed his first name to Morris. When he and Rose had a second son, on September 26, 1898, they named him Jacob Gershwine. Yet they always called him George, and they soon settled on another family name, Gershvin.

Morris Gershvin wanted to own his own business and to grow wealthy in the United States. He opened one establishment after another: a bakery, a cigar store, a billiard parlor, restaurants, and bathhouses. Instead of striking it rich, though, Morris Gershvin usually went out of business. There were times when Rose pawned her diamond ring to maintain the family's middle-class way of life.

The Gershvins seemed always to be moving to a different East Side apartment. Morris liked to live close to his place of business, and landlords commonly offered new tenants a free month's rent. When George was born, the family was living briefly in suburban Brooklyn. They moved twenty-eight times before he was eighteen.

George Gershwin referred to his father as a "very easy-going, humorous philosopher." Morris Gershvin was a softhearted man who always gave change to panhandlers. In later years, when he bought an automobile, he avoided

George's older brother, Izzy Gershvin, was more fascinated with books than music.

honking the horn, fearing he might startle the driver in front of him. Rose, in contrast, was ambitious and hard-working. She labored alongside Morris in his businesses, usually keeping the books, and had little time left to watch the children. A hired nurse looked after Arthur and Frances, the youngest boy and girl, while Izzy studied and George skated.

George spent less time playing on the street after he started taking piano lessons. His first teacher was a neighborhood woman, Miss Green. But soon he could play as well as she could, and he had to find another instructor. He went through three teachers before he started studying with Mr. Goldfarb, who taught him to play rousing versions of melodies from the great operas.

As a young teenager, George went to concerts with Izzy. He kept all of the concert programs in a scrapbook, along with newspaper articles he cut out about music and musicians. He took a summer job when he was thirteen playing the piano at a resort in the Catskill Mountains in upstate New York. During the school year, he performed with a community group called the Beethoven Society Orchestra. One of the men in the orchestra advised George to find a better teacher, and he recommended Charles Hambitzer.

Hambitzer was a fine pianist who was dedicated to his students. He gladly taught young people from poor families if he thought they showed ability—even if they couldn't afford to pay. At his first meeting with George,

Hambitzer asked the boy to play something he had learned with Mr. Goldfarb. "I rubbed my fingers and dived into the Overture to *William Tell*," Gershwin said. In the opera *Wilhelm Tell*, by Gioacchino Rossini, a marksman must shoot an apple on his son's head with a bow and arrow.

Hambitzer waited for his pupil to finish. Then he joked that they should find Mr. Goldfarb and shoot him—"and not with an apple on his head, either!" Hambitzer could hear George's talent beneath the unnecessary flourishes he had learned from Goldfarb, and took him on as a student.

Over the next few years, Hambitzer taught George to play pieces by Frederic Chopin, Claude Debussy, and other great European composers. He sent George to another teacher, Edward Kilenyi, to learn music theory, which is the study of how music is constructed. Excitedly, Hambitzer wrote to his sister, "I have a new pupil who will make his mark in music if anybody will. The boy is a genius, without a doubt; he's just crazy about music and can't wait until it's time to take his lesson." The letter continued, "He wants to go in for this modern stuff, jazz and what not. But I'm not going to let him for a while. I'll see that he gets a firm foundation in the standard music first."

George had discovered that there were many places to hear music in New York. North of Fourteenth Street, a new kind of music called ragtime bounced out of the nightclubs of Harlem and the saloons of midtown Manhattan. Believed to have originated in St. Louis with African-American musicians such as Scott Joplin (1868-1917), ragtime had swept the nation at the turn of the twentieth century.

Lively, jumping, and complex, ragtime usually was played on a piano. As the pianist's left hand put out a steady beat, the right hand bounced around the keyboard to play a syncopated melody, one that stressed beats that would not usually be emphasized in European music. In ragtime, it often looked as though the pianist's left and right hands were playing two entirely different songs. George watched the ragtime musicians closely, looking for techniques to try in his own playing.

Ragtime was only one way in which African Americans had influenced popular music in the United States. In the nineteenth century, a type of music known as the blues had developed from spirituals and the chants of black field workers in the South. The blues often expressed sadness. Singers lamented about growing old and dying, losing love, working hard, and being poor. What really set the blues apart from other kinds of music, though, was the use of "blue notes." These sad-sounding notes were frequently played or sung out of tune to communicate strong emotion.

Another style of music was evolving when George Gershwin was young. Born in New Orleans, jazz was the daughter of the blues. Jazz musicians used blue notes and

George began studying music theory as a teenager with Edward Kilenyi.

syncopation to play with melodies. They stretched out notes to squeeze every bit of feeling from the music. In jazz, musicians improvise: They decide how to play a passage of music on the spur of the moment. In that way, they are able to talk to one another with their instruments.

Most Americans in the early twentieth century had never heard jazz, but they knew many popular songs. When a song became a hit, people who owned a phonograph could buy a recording of it. Many more, though, would buy the sheet music and learn to play the song themselves at home. Others might purchase the song on a perforated roll for use in a player piano.

A whole industry had arisen in New York City to fill the demand for popular songs that were easy to learn. Several music publishers did business on a stretch of West Twenty-eighth Street that came to be known as Tin Pan Alley. They employed songwriters to come up with melodies and lyrics, and "song pluggers" to play the new songs for customers. Many of Tin Pan Alley's songwriters could barely pick out a tune on a piano with one finger. Some who were very successful could not even read music! It is not surprising that most of the songs that came out of Tin Pan Alley were soon forgotten.

By age fifteen George Gershwin knew how to play "Alexander's Ragtime Band," by Irving Berlin, and the other hit songs of the day. He had also started writing songs of his own. His first known song was called "Since I Found You." He never finished it, but he remembered the melody all his life and often played it for fun. He also wrote "Ragging the Traumerei," a ragtime version of a piece by the German composer Robert Schumann that he had learned studying with Charles Hambitzer.

Music was George's calling. He wanted to spend his life writing and performing. Rose Gershvin had other plans. Although George showed no talent in that direction, his mother decided that he should become an accountant. She enrolled him in the High School of Commerce, a school with a business curriculum. George played the piano at morning assemblies, but he hated high school and received terrible grades.

One day in March 1914, he walked into the offices of Jerome H. Remick and Company, the largest music publisher on Tin Pan Alley, and auditioned for a job as a song plugger. The manager offered to hire him right away after hearing him play, at a salary of fifteen dollars a week.

George went home and told his parents that his school days were over. As he expected, his mother had a fit. But Morris Gershvin breathed a sigh of relief, thinking that George just might amount to something after all.

Chapter Two

Lucky Break

Tin Pan Alley was full of pianos. The music publishers doing business there had divided their offices into long rows of cubicles. A song plugger sat in each cubicle, ready to run through the company's tunes for anyone wanting to hear them. Some stars and producers of the stage came every day to hear the newest songs.

George Gershvin quickly gained a reputation as Remick's best piano player. But because he had so much talent, running through the same songs over and over soon bored him. At every opportunity he livened up his workday by improvising at the piano, inventing tricky arrangements of the simple Tin Pan Alley songs. Often a crowd formed around George's cubicle to hear the show that he put on.

Fred and Adele Astaire, a teenaged brother and sister who were hoofers, or professional dancers, stopped in frequently at Remick's. The Astaires and George were about the same age, and they became friends. They shared their dreams about the future. When George said that he wanted to write songs, Fred confided that he hoped to be a big star. George asked him, "Wouldn't it be great if I could write a musical show and you could be in it?"

The public loved musical stage shows. Operettas, with their flowing, sentimental songs and European settings, had been popular since the nineteenth century, while musical comedies had just hit the scene. When George was young, the typical musical comedy was a patchwork of songs and dance routines stitched together with a weak plot about love. Characters tended to burst into song for no reason at all. It didn't matter if a song had anything to do with the show's plot, as long as the audience liked it. People also flocked to revues, which featured singing, dancing, and choruses of young women in colorful costumes. A revue had no plot. It tried to be timely by poking fun at current issues and employing the latest slang.

Irving Berlin, the writer of many well-known American songs, had scored some of the most successful musical comedies. He was the most famous popular composer of the era. Berlin had started his career as a singing waiter, and he could neither read nor write music. He came to George's cubicle one day and asked the young plugger to write down the notes for a song he had just thought up. "George took it down, and he played it so that I just didn't recognize it, it was so beautiful," Berlin said. "And I was impressed by this great pianist and I asked him what he was doing. He said he was trying to write."

George had shown some of his original tunes to his

employers, hoping to have them published. But the big shots at Remick's would barely look at them. Pluggers were paid to play songs and not to write them, they said.

So George knocked on other Tin Pan Alley office doors, and on March 1, 1916, he sold a song to Harry Von Tilzer, a competing music publisher. It was a bouncy little number with a long title: "When You Want 'em You Can't Get 'em, When You Got 'em You Don't Want 'em." Von Tilzer offered to pay George and Murray Roth, the boy who wrote the lyrics, the grand sum of one dollar. Later on they would receive one cent for every four copies of the sheet music that were sold. George's brown eyes lit up with delight as he envisioned huge earnings rolling in. Meanwhile, Murray Roth, who had better business sense, insisted that Von Tilzer give him fifteen dollars up front instead.

George waited for his riches to arrive, but he received nothing in the weeks that followed. Months went by, and George grew so impatient that he went back to Von Tilzer and asked for more money. "He handed me five dollars," Gershwin said. "And I never got a cent more from him."

George may not have grown rich, but he was far from poor at the time. He worked at a second job every Saturday, making music rolls for player pianos. He did this on a recording piano, an instrument equipped with a drum of paper inside. The drum turned as he played, and bits of carbon made marks on the paper, showing which keys he had pressed. The paper was then taken out of the piano, and holes were punched over the carbon markings to make a master roll. The piano-roll manufacturer made many copies of the master roll by machine.

George earned thirty-five dollars for every six master rolls that he completed. When he learned that his name would appear on some of the rolls, he changed his surname to Gershwin—to make it sound more like the name of his favorite comedian, Ed Wynn. Soon the rest of his family adopted the name Gershwin. Izzy went a step further and picked out a new first name, Ira.

The team of George Gershwin and Murray Roth sold a second song, but George wanted to do more. The next step on the pathway to success was to have a song interpolated, or inserted, in a show.

George dropped in on the songwriter Sigmund Romberg one day and played him one of his songs, hoping that Romberg would be impressed enough to use it in a musical show. Romberg disliked the song, but he admired George's skillful playing of it. He also liked the fact that the boy believed in himself. In his thick, Hungarian accent, Romberg asked George to help with the music for a new revue, *The Passing Show of 1916*.

George was elated when one of his songs made it into the score. He didn't even mind that Romberg received credit for composing it. He now felt so sure of his future that he quit his song-plugging job on March 17, 1917— and then realized that he had no idea what to do next.

He was not out of work for long. A nightclub manager

hired him to accompany singers and comedians in a dinner show. Walking out in front of an audience for the first time made him nervous, and his stomach did a few flips as he sat down at the piano. But the opening song went well, and he began to feel confident. Then the chorus started an elaborate song-and-dance routine, and George was horrified to see that his sheet music for the act was too messy to read. Hoping that no one would notice, he started to improvise.

He thought he had gotten away with it until a comedian stepped forward and signaled the chorus to be quiet. The comedian walked over to the piano, leaned close to George, and asked, "Who told you you were a piano player?" Laughter from the audience encouraged the comedian to go on. "You ought to be banging the drums," he said. George got up from the piano and left the theater, his face red with shame.

Soon, George had another job, playing at rehearsals for a new musical, *Miss 1917*. Two songwriters, Victor Herbert and Jerome Kern, had written the score for this show. Kern was one of the first Broadway composers to write songs that fit in with a show's plot. George recognized that his songs were more complex and melodic than the typical hits cranked out on Tin Pan Alley.

Jerome Kern and Victor Herbert argued during the rehearsals for *Miss 1917*. Each man wanted his own songs featured more prominently in the show. The feuding harmed the production, which critics called a disaster.

George worked with songwriter Jerome Kern on the musical *Miss 1917*.

George's work was finished once the show opened, though, and he concentrated on songwriting. He had a new job. A music publisher was paying him thirty-five dollars a week just to compose songs.

Anytime George had an idea for a song, he jotted it down in a notebook that he carried wherever he went. He often composed by improvising at the piano and writing down his best ideas, although he could store a great deal of music in his memory.

In 1917, after the United States entered World War I, most of the song pluggers on Tin Pan Alley were hammering out patriotic marches. The covers of sheet music from that year featured soldiers in uniform and flag-draped wives and sweethearts. As U.S. servicemen sailed across the Atlantic Ocean to help defeat the Central Powers, the Broadway composer George M. Cohan wrote the year's most memorable song, "Over There," reaffirming America's commitment to fight for victory.

But George Gershwin was so caught up in his work that he hardly noticed World War I. He was writing songs with titles such as, "I Was So Young (You Were So Beautiful)," and he was accompanying a popular singer, Nora Bayes, on a concert tour.

The war ended on November 11, 1918. The armistice was just one event in a year filled with emotional highs and lows for George Gershwin. His friend and teacher Charles Hambitzer died in 1918. It was also in 1918 that he had three songs interpolated in a show, *Ladies First.*

One was "The Real American Folk Song (Is a Rag)," with lyrics by Arthur Francis.

No one in the music business had ever heard of Francis, and Gershwin would only say that he was a college boy. In reality, Arthur Francis was George's brother Ira, who was not in college at all. Ira was trying his luck at writing lyrics and wanted to succeed on his own merit, without anyone knowing that he was related to George. He created his pseudonym from the names of his youngest siblings, Arthur and Frances.

In 1919, George Gershwin got what he called his first lucky break. He was hired to write the score for a new musical comedy, *La, La, Lucille*. With its plot about a dentist who must divorce his dancing-girl wife to receive an inheritance, *La, La, Lucille* was going to be "A New Up-to-the-Minute Musical Comedy of Class and Distinction," according to the advertisements.

Gershwin's boss, Alex Aarons, had given up selling clothing to work in show business. As the play's producer, Aarons had many responsibilities. He had to hire people, secure a theater, and obtain costumes, props, and scenery. It was his job to solve the many problems that were bound to crop up during rehearsals.

Aarons had heard many of Gershwin's songs, but he knew none of their titles. He had a way of letting George know which ones he wanted to hear, as Ira Gershwin observed: "Whisking his hand across George's shoulder [Aarons] would say, 'Play me the one that goes like *that*.'

Or, 'Play the tune that smells like an onion.' Or, '*You* know, the one that reminds me of the Staten Island Ferry.' "

La, La, Lucille opened in Boston, Massachusetts, on June 12, 1919, and the critics praised Gershwin's work. The music is "now vivacious and surprising of detail, and again harmoniously pleasing," stated a review in the *Boston Evening Transcript.*

Back in New York, Gershwin had dinner one night with a lyricist named Irving Caesar, who was always full of ideas. Over their steaks, they talked about the latest hit songs, especially "Hindustan," which had a frisky beat that was just right for the one-step, a popular dance.

Caesar asked, why don't we write a one-step of our own? Their song could be about an American subject rather than a foreign locale, he said. Gershwin liked his friend's suggestion, so as soon as they finished eating, he and Caesar hurried to the Gershwin home to get to work. The Gershwins had left the Lower East Side and now lived in a roomy apartment on 144th Street, in the northern part of the city.

Morris Gershwin had invited a few friends in to play cards that night. Some of them complained about the noise George and Irving were making at the piano, claiming that it disturbed their concentration. They were the players who were losing. The winners told the songwriters to continue, because the music was bringing them luck.

It took no more than fifteen minutes for George and

Irving to finish their song. Morris Gershwin liked it so much that he went to find some tissue paper and a comb. While George played the piano and Irving sang, Morris hummed through the comb wrapped in tissue, making it sound like a kazoo.

The listening public first heard Gershwin and Caesar's one-step, "Swanee," during a spectacular show celebrating the opening of New York's Capitol Theatre, the largest theater in the world at that time. A stage full of people sang the song while sixty women danced, wearing electric lights on their shoes.

The sheet music for "Swanee" was displayed in the theater's lobby for patrons to buy on their way out. But to the songwriters' dismay, hardly anyone wanted it. Sometimes Gershwin or Caesar bought a copy, thinking that if people saw someone else buying the song, they might want it, too.

No one did—until Gershwin had another lucky break. The singing star Al Jolson heard "Swanee" and decided to sing it in his current show, *Sinbad*. He also recorded it. Now the public went crazy for "Swanee," buying up 2.5 million copies of the sheet music. People played Jolson's record in America and in Europe. George Gershwin would never write a more popular song.

Chapter Three

A Kaleidoscope of America

George Gershwin's career was off and running. He was the right composer at the right time. His music captured the excitement of the 1920s.

Between 1920 and 1924, Gershwin wrote the scores for George White's *Scandals*, a series of revues. George White was appearing as a dancer in *Miss 1917* when he and Gershwin met. Now, he produced a new show each year containing skits and songs that found humor in modern life. Radio had just come into people's homes in 1920, so Gershwin wrote a song for George White called "Tune in to J.O.Y." He wrote "Mah-Jongg" about the Chinese game that had become a fad.

The most popular song that Gershwin wrote for George White's *Scandals* was "I'll Build a Stairway to Paradise." Gershwin remembered the fabulous way this song was staged. "Two circular staircases surrounded the orchestra on the stage, leading high up into theatrical paradise," he said. "Mr. White had draped fifty of his most beautiful girls in a black patent-leather material which brilliantly reflected the spotlights." The women danced on the staircase while they sang the song.

"I'll Build a Stairway to Paradise" was the first song written for the musical theater that used blue notes. Even more unusual, though, was a short operatic piece that Gershwin wrote for the 1922 *Scandals*. Titled "Blue Monday," it was a melodrama set among the African Americans of New York's Harlem that promised to be a saga of "love, hate, passion, [and] jealousy," according to its prologue.

Gershwin composed the music for "Blue Monday" on a piano and filled it with the blues. Will Vodery, an African-American composer who worked on Broadway, orchestrated the piece. In other words, Vodery took Gershwin's piano music and rewrote it for the various instruments in an orchestra. A lyricist named Buddy De Sylva wrote the libretto, or lyrics, for the mini-opera.

There were no African Americans in the cast of George White's *Scandals*. Rather than hire black singers, White asked some of the cast members to perform "Blue Monday" in dark makeup called blackface. It was common for white singers and actors to impersonate African Americans on the stage in Gershwin's time. Even a big star like Al Jolson frequently sang in blackface.

George Gershwin had a terrible case of nervous indigestion the first time an audience heard "Blue Monday." The public's reaction to the work can hardly have made him feel any better. Audiences were used to laughing at performers in blackface, which was a standard comedy prop. Now they were confused by the show's sad ending, which left them in no mood to enjoy the rest of George White's revue. White pulled the experiment in opera after a single performance in New York.

One person who liked the jazz opera was Paul Whiteman, George White's orchestra conductor. Sometime in 1923, he told Gershwin that he was thinking about putting together a jazz concert and asked him to compose something for the event. Gershwin declined, because he had too many other things to do. He was writing the score for a musical comedy, *Sweet Little Devil*, and he was working with an opera singer, Eva Gauthier, on a recital she was planning.

Gauthier's fans had learned to expect unusual programs from her, and in November 1923, she didn't disappoint them. After she sang some songs by composers from the seventeenth and nineteenth centuries, a dark-haired, nervous young man joined her on stage in a tuxedo. It was George Gershwin. The second part of the program consisted of modern songs, and Gershwin played while Gauthier sang.

They began with "Alexander's Ragtime Band," by Irving Berlin. A reporter for the *New York World* who was in the theater that night noted that "The audience was as much fun to watch as the songs were to hear..." At first, the listeners acted as if they were too cultured to enjoy such fare. But after hearing some of Gershwin's own songs performed, the writer stated, the audience "ended by surrendering completely to the alluring rhythms of our own folk music." In every row, heads were nodding, fingers and feet were tapping. For her encore, Gauthier sang a Gershwin song called "Do It Again." "Even then her hearers were not satisfied," the writer said, "and she had to do it again." A critic for another newspaper noted that Gershwin had ushered in "the age of sophisticated jazz."

The Gershwin songs and Gauthier's singing of them were not exactly jazz. There was little improvisation in the performance—Gershwin and Gauthier stuck to the music as it was written. But the audience had responded to the composer's blue notes and syncopated rhythms because they sounded new. Next the public would get a real lesson in modern music.

On January 4, 1924, Gershwin was at a billiard parlor on Broadway with lyricist Buddy De Sylva. Ira sat near them, reading aloud from a newspaper. Ira read that Paul Whiteman was putting on a concert at Aeolian Hall in New York City on February 12. Whiteman was now calling himself the King of Jazz, and his concert was going to be *An Experiment in Modern Music.* A number of composers were at work on pieces for the concert, including George Gershwin, who was writing a jazz concerto.

That was news to George Gershwin, who had never promised to do such a thing! He called up Whiteman to say that he couldn't possibly write anything in thirty-nine days, but Whiteman convinced him that he could. It wouldn't have to be a long, serious piece, Whiteman said. Instead, Gershwin could write something loose and lively—something like a rhapsody. In a rhapsody, composers traditionally have given their imaginations freedom to explore heroic or nationalistic feelings. But any emotion or idea could inspire a rhapsody.

Gershwin agreed to write a rhapsody, and immediately his own imagination went to work. He often heard music in the noise of modern life. And as he traveled from New York to Boston for the out-of-town tryout of *Sweet Little Devil*, he heard music in the rattle of the train's wheels moving over the track. Suddenly, parts of the unwritten rhapsody played inside his head. "I heard it as a sort of musical kaleidoscope of America," he wrote, "of our vast melting pot, of our incomparable national pep, our blues, our metropolitan madness." The scenes suggested by Gershwin's music would shift rapidly, just as the image seen through a kaleidoscope changes with a twist of the wrist.

Gershwin wrote the rhapsody at a furious pace, tuning out his family's card games and conversations. He never could say for sure how quickly he worked. "I wrote it in ten days," he claimed in 1926. But later he said, "I don't believe the rhapsody took more than three weeks to write, off and on."

A part of his mind was always working on the piece,

Paul Whiteman, "the King of Jazz," was an influential musician during the first half of the twentieth century.

even when he was doing other things. One day, he was seated at the piano, playing for enjoyment and not even thinking about the rhapsody. "All at once," he said, "I heard myself playing a theme that must have been haunting me inside, seeking outlet." Ira had heard George playing the new melody and urged him to include it in the rhapsody. George took his brother's advice and placed the theme at the climax of the work.

Ira also came up with a name for the piece. Ira loved art and had just seen an exhibit of paintings by the American artist James McNeill Whistler. Whistler, who was deeply interested in color and design, gave his paintings titles such as *Nocturne in Black and Gold*. The famous painting known popularly as *Whistler's Mother* is actually *Arrangement in Black and Grey No. 1*. When Ira heard the blue notes in George's composition, he suggested the title *Rhapsody in Blue*. After all, what could be more American than the blues?

The finished rhapsody would be a piece for piano and jazz band, but Gershwin only had time to compose it for the piano. He wrote a two-piano version representing the parts for the soloist and band. Ferde Grofé, a member of Whiteman's band, did the orchestration. Grofé arranged one of the piano parts for the instruments in the jazz band, which included violins, string basses, trumpets, trombones, French horns, drums, saxophones, clarinet, and banjo. Later on, Grofé would adapt the rhapsody for a symphony orchestra, creating the version heard most often today. Even with Grofé's help, Gershwin had no time to finish the soloist's part, which he planned to play himself in the concert. When the time came, he would improvise.

Snow fell the day of the concert. That afternoon the musicians were backstage at Aeolian Hall, waiting for the audience to take their seats. Paul Whiteman, worried that no one would show up, peeked out the front door to see what was happening at the box office. To his surprise, he saw men and women lined up in the snow, pushing toward the door. Whiteman imagined for a moment that be was in the wrong place, thinking that people only behaved this way at a baseball game or a boxing match, and not at a concert. But then he recognized the songwriter Victor Herbert in the crowd, and he knew he was in a concert hall.

Soon, nearly all of the 1,300 seats were filled. All kinds of musicians had come. Tin Pan Alley songwriters sat beside vaudeville performers and opera stars. John Philip Sousa, famous for writing marches, was there, and so was the great Russian composer Sergei Rachmaninoff. Several newspapers had sent writers to report on the event. Everyone was curious about the new music that Whiteman promised to offer.

The bandleader had said that he was going to trace the development of modern music from the roots of jazz through the present day. So when the concert started with "Livery Stable Blues," a hit song from 1917 and not really an example of early jazz, the audience started to wonder what Whiteman was up to. Popular dance tunes came next, and people grew restless. Nothing new or interesting had been offered so far. Audience members yawned or looked at their watches. Some headed for the exits. The *Experiment in Modern Music* was turning out to be a bore.

Then, George Gershwin stepped onstage. His hair was slicked back, and his face was flushed with excitement. He was dressed smartly in a black jacket, gray trousers, and spats. He sat at the piano, Whiteman raised his baton, and music history was made.

At first, the only sound in the hushed concert hall was a flutter from a single clarinet. It was the sound of something awakening, of eyelids blinking open in the first light of day. The clarinetist played a glissando, sliding from a low note to a high one, as if the waking creature were stretching.

A fragment of melody, bluesy, relaxed, and sure, seemed to strut through the hall. Gershwin had invoked the spirit of the modern age, and its distinctive melody would drift in and out of his rhapsody, played now by the clarinet and now by the piano.

All at once, the entire band played, and the audience was delighted. They heard music that sounded like the machinery in factories, loud and pulsing and productive. The people who had been about to leave hurried back to their seats.

Whiteman's jazz band and Gershwin's piano played

alternately and then together. When Gershwin finished his solo improvisations, he nodded to let Whiteman know that it as time for the band to take over.

Suddenly, the music slowed and became flowing and melodious. It seemed now to change its viewpoint on America, to turn away from tall buildings and industry in order to survey miles of wheat and corn, mountain ranges, and wilderness. But civilization was never very far away. Soon, the piano suggested the clickety-clack of a moving train, and the horns became the whistle of the locomotive straining to pull it forward. The rhapsody picked up speed and came to its conclusion with cymbals clashing. A new day in American music had arrived.

As soon as Gershwin played the last, loud chord, the audience let loose with wild applause for the vibrant new rhapsody and its twenty-five-year-old composer. Gershwin, Whiteman, and the band members bowed again and again. "At half-past five on the afternoon of February 12, 1924, we took our fifth curtain call," Paul Whiteman said.

All of the critics had something to say about the *Rhapsody in Blue*. One wrote, "If this way lies the path toward the upper development of American modern music into a high art form, then one can heartily congratulate Mr. Gershwin on his disclosure of some of the possibilities." Another critic commented, "The Rhapsody hinted at something new, something that has not hitherto been said in music."

Not everyone felt optimistic after hearing Gershwin's piece. Some critics felt that it showed "structural uncertainty," that it suffered from "melodic and harmonic anemia." One writer even advised the public to "weep over the lifelessness of its melody and harmony, so derivative, so stale, so inexpressive."

What had Gershwin done to inspire such differing reactions? He had employed the sounds of jazz and the blues, two African-American musical styles, in a form of composition from the European tradition of classical music, the rhapsody. He had experimented with new combinations of notes to create his own harmonies. And he had brought the rhythms and instruments of popular song onto a concert stage.

Nothing like the *Rhapsody in Blue* had ever been written before. A few American composers, such as Louis Moreau Gottschalk (1829-1869), had incorporated American folk melodies in their music. But these composers had trained in Europe, and they wrote music similar to what European composers were writing.

Today the *Rhapsody in Blue* is performed in concerts regularly. But in the 1920s, scholars were debating about what contribution American composers could make to musical composition, if any. Most prominent people in the field, who were of northern European descent, pointed out that America lacked a long, distinguished cultural history like that of Europe. Only by following European examples could American composers hope to write anything worthwhile. And as for African-American music—why, it might corrupt "serious" music just as immigrants threatened to taint American society!

It was lucky for George Gershwin that most people were not stuffy experts. Ordinary Americans and Europeans alike loved the *Rhapsody in Blue* and wanted to hear it repeatedly. Paul Whiteman's band performed the piece eighty-four times in 1924, often with Gershwin at the piano. The record that Gershwin and Whiteman made together sold one million copies. The rhapsody was played so often over the next ten years that it earned Gershwin $250,000. Musicians arranged it for one piano, for two pianos, and for all sorts of combinations of instruments.

A year after the *Experiment in Modern Music* at Aeolian Hall, one of the critics who had been in the audience that day was still thinking back on the afternoon's music. Samuel Chotzinoff of the *New York World* wrote, "It remained for George Gershwin...to hitch the rhythm of the body with the sentiments of the heart and mind of the average present-day American."

Chapter Four

Composer? American?

"Swanee" had brought George Gershwin some acclaim. *Rhapsody in Blue* made him famous throughout the world. Gershwin slipped into the role of celebrity easily, as if it were a custom-tailored tuxedo. He was naturally outgoing and friendly, and he was relaxed and charming in crowds. The elegant hosts and hostesses of New York all wanted him as their guest.

Gershwin enjoyed parties, and he attended many of them. If his hosts owned a piano, he spent most of the evening playing music. Stylishly dressed and holding an expensive cigar between his teeth, he liked nothing better than to put on an informal show. When a song ended, the crowd assembled around the piano called out, "Go on! Play some more!" Gershwin needed little persuasion. He flashed his listeners a smile and plunged into something new.

Gershwin's delight in playing his own music provoked a friend to comment, "An evening with Gershwin is a Gershwin evening." Another friend, the pianist Oscar

Levant, asked one time, "George, if you had it to do all over again, would you still fall in love with yourself?" Gershwin laughed at such comments and took them in stride, although the words were often tinged with envy.

Show-business personalities and visiting foreign musicians often dropped in at the posh parties. But the gatherings Gershwin liked best took place on Saturday nights at the small apartment of teacher Lou Paley and his wife, Emily. The Paleys, who were on a tight budget, served cookies to their guests instead of hors d'ouevres. No one minded, because they came to hear music and have a good time. Even Ira, who would rather stay home reading than go out, showed up sometimes at the Paleys' place. He sat in the background and smiled as he listened to his brother play. "Ira's a hard man to get out of an easy chair," a friend of his once remarked.

A lyricist named Howard Dietz lived downstairs from the Paleys in 1924. Every Saturday night, pounding on the floor above caused the chandelier on his ceiling to shake wildly. He and his wife worried that the chandelier might fall down.

One Saturday night, a desperate Dietz went upstairs to beg the Paleys to stop whatever they were doing. "Someone opened the door carefully and put fingers to lips, cautioning me not to disturb the music," Dietz stated. "About forty people were sitting on the floor around the grand piano at which a dark chap was playing and singing..." Dietz sat down, too, and after a while his wife came up to find out what had happened to him. "I went to the door, put my fingers to my lips and motioned to her to come in and sit down," Dietz wrote. "We stopped bothering about our chandelier. But every Saturday night from then on we went upstairs and attended a sacred concert by George Gershwin."

Gershwin used his time at parties to work on new material. Whether a get-together was simple or sumptuous, the guests often heard his newest songs.

As soon as he was finished with the *Rhapsody in Blue*, Gershwin hurried to England to write the music for a show called *Primrose*, which was a huge success in London. One English newspaper mentioned that some of the songs in *Primrose* had lyrics by the composer's "sister Ira!" Ira Gershwin now felt ready to drop the name Arthur Francis and take credit for his work.

George Gershwin never rested while he was in England. He went to tennis matches at Wimbledon, played golf, attended dinner parties nearly every night, and shopped for presents to bring back to New York. He also toyed at the piano, coming up with a quirky melody full of what he called "misplaced accents."

And then he dashed home to score a new musical comedy for the producer Alex Aarons. Aarons had hired both George and Ira to write the songs for *Lady, Be Good!*, starring George's old friends Fred and Adele Astaire. Aarons was taking a big chance, because George and Ira had never written an entire score together, and the

Astaires had never starred in a Broadway show.

Fred and Adele were to play a brother and sister named Dick and Susie Trevor who have lost their money and their home. In the hope of snagging a rich husband, Susie pretends to be a wealthy Mexican widow. The silly, contrived plot is filled with cases of mistaken identity, but the show ends happily, with both Dick and Susie marrying for love.

The Gershwins wrote songs for the show that tied in with the plot or that revealed the characters' thoughts and feelings. For example, their song "Hang on to Me," dealt with the bond of love between a brother and sister, like that of Dick and Susie Trevor.

The Astaires were known best as dancers, so the show had to contain some peppy dance tunes. George brought out the melody he had played with in England, the one with the odd accents. An exasperated Ira asked, "For God's sake, George, what kind of lyric do you write to a rhythm like that?" Ira mulled over the melody for a few days, finally deciding it had a fascinating rhythm—and that is the title he gave to the song.

Settling on a title was just the first small step in writing the lyrics to "Fascinating Rhythm," as it was for any song. "It was a tricky rhythm for those days, and it took me several days to decide on the rhyme scheme," Ira explained. At last, he came up with lyrics that evoked the propulsive energy of the 1920s and the interest in jazz and dance crazes that characterized the decade.

Once the song was written, the Astaires learned to sing it and worked out a dance routine. Fred Astaire revealed how Gershwin helped them out when they had trouble with their dance. "Adele and I were stuck for an exit step. We had the routine set but needed a climax wow step," he said. "For days I couldn't find one." In desperation, he asked George for an idea. Gershwin proposed that the dancers do something called "traveling." He demonstrated what he had in mind, tilting his head back, pulling with his arms, and kicking. Fred and Adele should do this, he said, while crossing in front of each other and moving offstage. "There was a lot going on, and when George suggested traveling, we didn't think it was possible," Astaire noted. "It was the perfect answer to our problem, however, this suggestion by hoofer Gershwin, and it turned out to be a knockout applause puller."

Lady, Be Good! opened in Philadelphia in November 1924, and it was a hit. The show made stars of the Astaires, and it launched one of the most successful songwriting teams in the history of the American musical theater, George and Ira Gershwin. Between 1925 and 1933, the brothers would collaborate on thirteen shows, writing hundreds of songs together.

For George Gershwin, writing songs was now only one aspect of his career. He continued to write serious music and to be a concert pianist. In the spring of 1925, Walter Damrosch, conductor of the New York Symphony Orchestra, commissioned him to write a piece of music for the orchestra to perform.

Gershwin was eager to start a symphonic piece that would reaffirm his talent. "Many people thought the Rhapsody was only a happy accident," he said. He was determined to write more and better works, "to show them that there was plenty more where that had come from." He decided to write a piano concerto, which is a work for piano and orchestra. Ira remarked that his brother was brave to take on such a challenge. George would first have to study the concerto form, about which he knew little. George Gershwin liked to claim that after he signed a contract with Walter Damrosch, he bought a book to learn what a concerto was. In reality, he purchased a textbook on orchestration. He needed to arrange the concerto for all of the instruments in a symphony orchestra. This task alone was a major undertaking.

Gershwin still did most of his composing at home, but home was becoming a hectic place. There were frequent card games, and friends were constantly stopping by. He rented two rooms at a hotel and tried to work in peace on the concerto and on two musicals that he was scoring. Even there, though, friends and relatives kept popping in.

A pianist and composer named Ernest Hutcheson came to Gershwin's rescue. Hutcheson taught at the Chatauqua Institute, a summer music school in western New York State, and he invited Gershwin to spend some time there in the quiet woods. Hutcheson promised him a cabin all to himself, where he could work undisturbed.

The piano students at the Chatauqua Institute were so

excited to have a famous composer in residence that they had to struggle to obey Hutcheson's rule: No one could visit Gershwin's cabin before four o'clock. Each afternoon, as soon as the clock struck four, the little rustic shelter filled with young musicians. "George would good-naturedly play and sing to them for a treasured hour," Ernest Hutcheson stated.

Gershwin returned to the city at summer's end with half of the concerto tucked under his arm. His family had just moved into a five-story house on West 103rd Street, where they congregated around a billiard table on the first floor.

The kitchen was on this level, and Rose Gershwin was often found there cooking up her family's favorite meals. George especially liked the way she prepared lamb chops and the Russian beet soup called borscht. Many times, George joined his family around the kitchen table late at night to eat cornflakes and chat.

The Gershwins had plenty of room to spread out in their new house. On the second floor was a living room with two pianos as well as Rose and Morris's bedroom. Frances and Arthur slept on the third floor, and Ira claimed the fourth. George had the fifth floor to himself. He worked in a private music room that held a third piano.

S. N. Behrman, Gershwin's playwright friend, described a visit he made to the hectic Gershwin household. He wrote that no one answered the door when he rang the bell, but he could see people inside, so he let himself in. (The Gershwins never locked their door.)

"Three or four young men I had never seen before were sitting around the hall smoking," Berhman said. He saw a game under way in the billiard room but recognized none of the players. "I asked for George, or his brother Ira," Behrman said. "No one bothered to reply, but one of the young men made a terse gesture in the direction of the upper stories."

After riding an elevator to the second level, Behrman encountered another group of strangers who knew nothing about George and Ira. Arthur, who was on the third floor, claimed to know none of the people below. Behrman then rode to the fourth floor and called out for George or Ira.

At last, Ira shouted down to him from the top floor and invited him up to George's study. There, Behrman discovered Ira, George, and George's fox terrier, Tony. "Who under the sun are those fellows playing billiards on the first floor?" Behrman asked. "To tell you the truth, I don't know," Ira replied. "There's a bunch of fellows from down the street who've taken to dropping in here every night for a game."

George finished his composition in the relative peace and quiet of the fifth floor. He called it simply *Concerto in F*.

On December 3, 1925, George Gershwin and the New York Symphony Orchestra played the *Concerto in F* before the public for the first time. Gershwin had a case of "composer's stomach," the indigestion he felt whenever a work was premiered. His friends agreed among themselves that his stomachaches were due to nerves.

The people who filled Carnegie Hall to capacity on that cold, rainy day expected to hear something as startling and original as the *Rhapsody in Blue*. The music they heard was not quite what they had hoped for. Some liked it, while others did not.

Gershwin had used a structure that composers had employed for centuries when writing concertos. He had created three movements: The first fast-paced, the second slow, and the third fast again. Still, much of the concerto was pure Gershwin. Music suggesting the Charleston was heard in the first movement. The second began with a muted trumpet playing the blues. The rip-roaring third movement was "an orgy of rhythm," Gershwin said. With a rushing beat that sounded like a rapid pulse, the third movement conveyed a high-strung, jittery feeling. Listeners could almost see, in their minds, crowds of people hurrying along a Manhattan sidewalk. Once, then twice, the music hit a crescendo, or increase in volume. Cymbals clashed, a kettledrum pounded, and the concerto ended with a shiver of excitement—and a second one, and a third.

Songwriter Irving Berlin was one of the people who cheered Gershwin's concerto. He congratulated the composer, saying, "I am rooting hard for the success and glory you so richly deserve."

Samuel Chotzinoff, the writer who had called Gershwin

The composer Irving Berlin (right) was an avid fan of Gershwin's innovative music.

the voice of the present-day American, now had more praise for him. Of all those writing music in the 1920s, "He alone actually expresses us," Chotzinoff said. He called Gershwin "an instinctive artist," someone with an inborn talent to create.

But to most critics, the *Concerto in F* sounded less spontaneous than the *Rhapsody in Blue*. Despite its blue notes and Charleston rhythms, the concerto was "conventional, [and] trite," according to one music critic, and "at its worst, a little dull." Gershwin saw snobbishness in such comments, a refusal to take his music seriously because of its American roots. He vented some frustration in *Vanity Fair* magazine, when the editors asked him, in fun, to draft his epitaph. He wrote:

> Here lies the body of George Gershwin
> American Composer
> * * * *
> Composer?
> American?

The opinion of ordinary listeners was the one Gershwin valued most. He felt gratified when the audience responded to his concerto with cheers and spirited applause.

On the night of the premiere, Gershwin's friends threw a party in his honor and presented him with a gold cigarette case. Gershwin's friends now spent a lot of time discussing his future. Should he write only concert music from now on, or should he still write songs for Broadway shows? Should he begin intensive study in composition, or would too much education spoil his original approach to music? Everyone had an opinion. "Pursue musical studies and forge on with large scale orchestral works," counseled the conductor Walter Damrosch. "Further study will cramp your style; stick with songs," countered lyricist Buddy De Sylva.

Gershwin was still working with Edward Kilenyi, the theory teacher Charles Hambitzer had recommended years earlier. (He would continue his musical studies with Kilenyi and others for most of his life.) He listened patiently to his friends' advice, but saw no reason to choose one course or another. Writing for the theater, he said, was "agreeable and remunerative"—it was fun, and it paid well. Serious composition allowed him to grow. He would keep on doing both.

Chapter Five

Carefree

At age twenty-seven George Gershwin called himself "a fairly busy young composer." His schedule for December 1925 reveals just how busy he was. The *Concerto in F* had its premiere on December 3. *Tip-Toes*, a musical with lyrics by Ira Gershwin, opened on Broadway on the 28th. The next day, Paul Whiteman staged a revival of the operatic piece "Blue Monday." Finally, on December 30, Gershwin attended the opening of *Song of the Flame*, another show he had scored.

And then there were new projects to start. He composed a series of preludes—short works for piano—in 1926. He and Ira wrote the songs for *Oh, Kay!*, a musical comedy with a plot about rum-running, or smuggling whiskey, into the United States.

Oh, Kay! contained one of the Gershwins best-loved ballads, "Someone to Watch Over Me." While the show was being rehearsed in Philadelphia, Gershwin came up with an idea. He ran out to a toyshop and bought a rag doll with long, floppy limbs. He thought that the show's star, Gertrude Lawrence, should sing the song to the doll, as if she were confiding in the comical little toy. Lawrence gave it a try, and once again, Gershwin's advice about performing turned out to be good. The musical number stopped the show—the actors had to wait several minutes for the applause to end before they could continue. Audience members told their friends about the unusual scene, and they remembered "Someone to Watch Over Me."

Gershwin tried something different himself when he wrote the songs for *Oh, Kay!*. To give the music a unified sound, he composed much of it using the pentatonic scale. A scale is a series of notes progressing from low to high, or high to low. Most Western music employs major or minor scales, which consist of seven notes. The pentatonic, or five-note, scale is used most often in the music of China, Africa, and Polynesia, and in some Native American music. The black keys on a piano represent the pentatonic scale.

In 1926, the year the Gershwins scored *Oh, Kay!*, Ira married Leonore Strunsky, who was Emily Paley's sister. Leonore came to live in the offbeat Gershwin household. Although George had many girlfriends, he would never marry. Music always came first in his heart. If he wasn't talking about it, he was thinking about it. Women stopped seeing him once they understood this fact. "He never made me feel needed," said one of his former girlfriends.

On one occasion, a woman George had been dating

called him to say that she was giving up on him, and that she planned to marry someone else. George admitted to Ira as he hung up the phone, "I would be heartbroken— if only I weren't so terribly busy."

The closest relationship in George Gershwin's life was his bond with Ira. The brothers were work partners and best friends, despite their differences.

Like many quiet people, Ira Gershwin was a good listener. Increasingly, he paid attention to the way Americans used words in everyday speech. He fashioned song lyrics from the slang and quirky pronunciations of his time. In 1927, Ira noticed that people living fast-paced city lives tended to speak so quickly that their words ran together. He mimicked this tendency in a love song written with George called "'S Wonderful."

Ira normally was even-tempered, but he became riled whenever someone got his lyrics wrong. "Don't ever let Ira hear you say, 'It's Wonderful,' " George warned.

With Ira's clever lyrics and George's sophisticated melody, "'S Wonderful" was one of the hit songs from *Funny Face*, another show starring the Astaires. *Funny Face* was a typical 1920s musical with a fluffy, humorous plot. Adele Astaire played a young woman with a vivid imagination who cannot resist making up details when writing in her diary. When a thief accidentally steals the diary along with some jewels, other people read the young woman's accounts, and a confusing chain of events follows.

Lighthearted plots like this one matched the public's optimism. The United States was at peace and prospering, and many Americans believed that everyone had a chance to get rich. People bought radios, vacuum cleaners, and washing machines. In the past, families had saved their money until they had enough cash to pay for an expensive item. Now, they bought things in a new way, by making monthly payments on the installment plan.

Many men and women had no fear of getting into debt because they expected to earn a fortune in the stock market. One million people from varied walks of life—business executives, cattle ranchers, ministers, home-makers—were so sure of a bright financial future that they purchased stocks on credit, planning to pay for them with their later profits. It often seemed that all eyes were on Wall Street in New York City, the financial center of the United States.

Some people were leery of the widespread optimism. One such person was George S. Kaufman, a playwright who had written a number of popular comedies. Tall, disheveled, and gloomy, Kaufman had a biting wit and a talent for satire. In 1927, he turned his attention to politics, writing the script for an anti-war musical, *Strike Up the Band*. Kaufman was a pacifist, and his script showed war to be foolish and patriotism to be misguided.

Strike Up the Band begins with the United States going to war with Switzerland over cheese. Americans had shunned all things German during World War I. Now they go after anything Swiss. Copies of the novel *Swiss Family Robinson* are removed from libraries. People are forbidden to wear Swiss watches. Unlike all musical comedies that came before it, *Strike Up the Band* has no happy ending. The show ends with the Americans preparing for another war—a confrontation with the Soviet Union over caviar.

The Gershwins wrote the songs for this strange show although they still had little interest in politics. They believed that no playwright was funnier or smarter than George S. Kaufman, and they created songs that deepened his satire. The title song was one Gershwin number with an ironic twist. It sounded like a stirring march, but its words poked fun at military songs.

George and Ira worked on *Strike Up the Band* in a house they rented for the summer in Ossining, New York, away from the stifling city. They wrote at night and entertained friends and family members during the day. George won many games of croquet on the lush lawn surrounding the house. He also bought a car, and he enjoyed zipping back and forth between Ossining and Manhattan. Ira learned to drive, too, but he soon decided that he could not deal with traffic. Leonore did all of the couple's driving from then on.

Despite George and Ira's imaginative work, *Strike Up the Band* was a flop. It "laid an egg," as people in the theater say, playing for only two weeks in New York. Most people in the 1920s were tired of rehashing World

War I, and the opinions put forth in the show bothered them. The audience members had fought overseas, or they had supported the war effort at home. They wondered, did Kaufman and the Gershwins expect them to laugh at themselves?

George Gershwin refused to dwell on either failure or success. Like all people who love their work, he looked ahead to what he would be doing next. His agile mind came up with ideas wherever he went.

In March 1928, George, Ira, Leonore, and Frances Gershwin left for a three-month trip to Europe. They visited England, France, Germany, and Austria. Everywhere they went the European music world honored George with luncheons and receptions. He picked the brains of the composers he met, eager to learn everything he could about writing music.

Gershwin loved Paris. He dragged Ira along on sightseeing trips and managed to get his stay-at-home brother to the top of the famed Eiffel Tower. At 984 feet, the tower was taller than the sixty-six-story Woolworth Building in New York. Ira liked the ride up in an elevator just fine, and the view from the top was not to be missed. But after walking down thirty-eight flights of stairs to the sidewalk, he was full of complaints. "Boy how my legs trembled when we finally got to the street," he noted in his journal. "It took me three blocks to get them straightened out."

Paris, in turn, was crazy about George Gershwin.

Every orchestra in the city seemed to be playing the *Rhapsody in Blue*. The Gershwins attended a ballet performed to the piece, in which dancers wearing dazzling blue costumes acted out a struggle between jazz and classical music.

In Paris, George discovered a city of culture and style where he was surrounded by great art and historic architecture. He saw fashionable women and men strolling or dining along the wide boulevards, and he mingled with tourists and Parisians at bright, noisy nightclubs after dark. He heard a symphony in the sounds of the city's crowded streets. Even the taxi horns of Paris had a music all their own.

He collected his musical impressions of the city in a tone poem, *An American in Paris*. It was a piece of music "to be handled lightly, in the spirit in which many Americans come here, to play, carefree and happy," he said. A tone poem is a musical work that describes an idea, emotion, or event, just as a poem written in words does. *An American in Paris* evokes Gershwin's idea of a visitor strolling along the city's streets and taking in the atmosphere for the first time.

"The opening gay section is followed by a rich 'blues' with a strong rhythmic undercurrent," Gershwin said. "Our American friend, perhaps after strolling into a cafe and having a few drinks, has suddenly succumbed to a spasm of homesickness." According to Gershwin, after the blues section reaches a climax, "the spirit of the music returns to the vivacity and bubbling exuberance of the opening part with the impressions of Paris. Apparently the homesick American, having left the cafe and reached the open air, has downed his spell of the blues and once again is an alert spectator of Parisian life. At the conclusion the street noises and French atmosphere are triumphant."

In *An American in Paris*, as most orchestras play it today, musical instruments suggest the honking of French taxi horns. When Gershwin wrote his tone poem, though, he wanted the real thing. He took Mabel Schirmer, a cousin of the Paleys who lived in Paris, on a horn-hunting expedition. They visited one auto mechanic's shop after another, with Mabel translating for George, who did not speak French. At each garage, Gershwin tried out any taxi horns that the mechanic had lying around, selecting a variety of horns in different pitches. At the first performance of *An American in Paris*, on December 13, 1928, the audience heard actual French taxi horns being played on the New York stage.

The music critics either loved *An American in Paris* or they hated it. One called it "easily the best piece of modern music since Mr. Gershwin's *Concerto in F.*" Another ranted that Gershwin had composed "Nauseous claptrap" that was so "dull, patchy, thin, vulgar, long-winded and inane that the average movie audience would be bored by it."

Some people had the vision to look beyond the critical

debate and understand Gershwin's importance to the music of his age. "George Gershwin is a leader of young America in music," pronounced Otto Kahn, a wealthy supporter of the Metropolitan Opera, at a party honoring the composer. "In the rhythm, the melody, the humor, grace, the rush and sweep and dynamics of his compositions, he expresses the genius of young America." Gershwin's music would speak for Americans of all ages, Kahn said, once some of life's tragedies had deepened his knowledge of human experience.

But the idea that tragedy would ever touch George Gershwin was hard to accept. He led a charmed life that kept getting better. After the Gershwin family stopped living together in 1928, he moved to a penthouse, a luxurious apartment at the very top of a building at 33 Riverside Drive in Manhattan. From his windows, Gershwin looked out across the Hudson River at the dramatic cliffs known as the Palisades on New Jersey's shore.

Ira and Leonore were his next-door neighbors, and he still saw a lot of his parents, Frances, and Arthur. Frances remembered that he liked to drop in and bring them ice cream, although he usually ate much of it himself.

Gershwin filled his new home with modern furniture, and he invited his cousin Henry Botkin to come over and admire his decorating scheme. Botkin, who was an artist, said that the furniture looked great, but the walls were too bare. That one remark prompted George to go shopping for paintings. Soon, his living room and dining room featured works by such modern masters as Pablo Picasso, Paul Gaugin, and Thomas Hart Benton. Gershwin kept on buying paintings even after he had covered his walls, because he had developed a love of art. His collection would grow to include 144 works, mostly modern paintings and African statues. Gershwin liked art because it had qualities in common with music. As he explained, "Music is design—melody is line; harmony is color." He often paused in his musical work to contemplate a piece of art.

Ira presented George with a set of watercolor paints on his thirtieth birthday. Ira liked to sketch and paint, and now George took up the hobby. He immediately showed a talent for art and painted portraits of himself, his family, and his friends and acquaintances. He liked to paint late at night. When he could no longer stay awake, he propped up his unfinished work at the foot of his bed. That way, he would see it again first thing in the morning. Gershwin's paintings show an unusual amount of natural ability. Some art experts have speculated that if he had focused his energy on painting instead of music, he could have been one of America's foremost artists.

Chapter Six

Music in Many Voices

On January 14, 1930, the Times Square Theater presented a musical with songs by George and Ira Gershwin. The show was *Strike Up the Band*, the anti-war comedy that had failed in 1927. In this version the United States warred with Switzerland over chocolate, not cheese, and the war took place in a character's dream. This time the show was a hit.

A writer named Morrie Ryskind had softened George S. Kaufman's satire, which made it easier for audiences to accept. But the attitude of theatergoers had changed as well. Something had happened to tinge their 1920s optimism with cynicism and fear—the stock market crash of October 29, 1929, and the Great Depression that followed.

In the midst of the economic collapse people did what they could to survive. Funds were taken away from schools and used to finance welfare for destitute families. Charity soup kitchens fed the hungry, and clusters of flimsy shanties sheltered families on the outskirts of cities. "Brother, Can You Spare a Dime?", a tune from a Broadway musical called *Americana*, became the depression's unofficial theme song.

Like other working Americans, many people in show business had a rough time. Ticket sales declined, and half of New York's theaters closed. Actors, musicians, and stagehands lost their jobs. A volunteer group called the Stage Relief Fund raised money to help out-of-work theater people, while a performer named Selena Royale formed the Actors' Dinner Club, serving meals for a dollar. Anyone who could not pay was allowed to eat free. During one depression winter, the Actors' Dinner Club dished up 150,000 meals—most at no charge.

An occasional musical comedy could still draw audiences to Broadway, especially if George and Ira Gershwin wrote the songs. In October 1930, their show *Girl Crazy* had its premiere. It was about a wealthy young man from New York whose father sends him west to live among the cowboys, away from girls. Of course, he falls in love with the only woman in town.

Girl Crazy featured a newcomer to show business named Ethel Merman. The eighteen-year-old Merman belted out the Gershwins' song "I Got Rhythm" and became a star overnight. George's irresistible, upbeat tune and Ira's quick, catchy lyrics excited people and made them happy. The song has remained a favorite of musicians and listeners. Even today, jazz musicians often play "I Got Rhythm," improvising on the tune's chords.

Gershwin liked the song so well that he developed it into the *Variations on "I Got Rhythm"* (1933), a work for piano and orchestra that included saxophones, a banjo, and a Chinese gong. In the variations, Gershwin created several versions of his popular song, making it sound sorrowful at one time and joyous at another. Gershwin dedicated the variations to his brother Ira.

Girl Crazy was the Gershwins' last Broadway musical in the lighthearted 1920s style. Weeks after the show opened, they boarded a train for Hollywood, California, to write songs for a movie. In 1927, the Warner Brothers film studio had released the first motion picture with sound, *The Jazz Singer*, starring Al Jolson. Audiences actually could hear Jolson singing several songs, and the film contained two scenes with spoken dialogue. Sound technology improved rapidly, and soon every movie studio was turning out full-length "talking pictures." Gangster films and musicals were the two most popular types of talkies.

The Gershwins wrote the score for *Delicious*, one of the earliest movie musicals. *Delicious* was filmed in California, but its story was set in Manhattan. The plot concerns a woman from Scotland named Heather who enters the United States illegally. The Gershwins devised a long musical scene for the film called "Welcome to the Melting Pot," which depicts Heather's dream on the night before her ship reaches New York. Heather greets eight Uncle Sams, Mr. Ellis of Ellis Island, and the Statue of Liberty.

The team of George and Ira Gershwin composed the score for the 1930 hit *Girl Crazy*.

The poor-but-beautiful Heather falls in love with a rich American but soon has to flee from immigration officers. Before being rescued by her new boyfriend, she roams the streets of New York, believing she is about to be deported. Gershwin wrote an eight-minute piece of music to serve as the soundtrack for this scene. For some time, Gershwin had wanted to compose a work that captured the spirit of Manhattan. In this short piece, the music blends with sounds of the city, including the calls of newsboys and the noise of riveting from construction projects such as the Empire State Building that was being built at the corner of Thirty-fourth Street and Fifth Avenue.

Gershwin thought about calling the piece *Manhattan Rhapsody*, or possibly *Rhapsody in Rivets*. After he brought the music back to New York and worked on it some more, he titled it *Second Rhapsody*. The movie producers had not expected him to compose something so ambitious for the film, but as Gershwin explained, "Nearly everybody comes back from California with a western tan and a pocketful of moving-picture money. I decided to come back with both those things and a serious composition."

He had come back to work on another musical. George S. Kaufman and Morrie Ryskind were at work on a second satire, and they wanted the Gershwins to write the songs for this new show. Kaufman and Ryskind spent sixteen days in a hotel room in Atlantic City, New Jersey, writing the first act of their play, *Of Thee I Sing*. As soon as the Gershwins read the script, they agreed to work on the project.

Of Thee I Sing lampooned national elections. It followed the campaign of John P. Wintergreen, a fictional candidate for president. Wintergreen's party takes no stand on political issues, so he runs on a platform of love. He announces that if elected, he will marry the winner of a beauty contest.

Wintergreen wins the election, but there is one catch. He has fallen in love with a campaign worker, a woman named Mary Turner, and he marries her instead. The marriage brings the United States to the brink of war with France, because the beauty contest winner is of French descent. Wintergreen is about to be impeached for breaking his promise.

The crisis is resolved when Mary gives birth to twins. Congress has never impeached a new father and does not wish to do so now. The vice president, Alexander Throttlebottom, marries the beauty queen, because the Constitution states that if a president cannot fulfill his duties, the vice president must do so in his place.

Of Thee I Sing is full of humor and satire. For example, campaign workers carry signs expressing people's real frustration with government, such as, "Vote for Prosperity and See What You Get." The vice president is shown to be so unimportant that no one can remember his name.

Kaufman and Ryskind worried that the American

people might take offense at their use of a line from the patriotic song "America" as the title of their play. Ira Gershwin made them more nervous by adding the slang endearment "baby" to a lyric taken from the revered song.

The playwrights need not have worried. As soon as *Of Thee I Sing* opened in New York, on December 26, 1931, the song was on everyone's lips. People who had seen the show, as well as those who had not, sang the title song to one another. Crowds flocked to the Music Box Theater, where the play was being performed, and gave the cast a standing ovation every night.

Of Thee I Sing became the first musical comedy to win the Pulitzer Prize for Drama, in 1932. The judges gave the prize to Kaufman, Ryskind, and Ira Gershwin, but not to George. The prize honored the writers of words, the judges said, and not music. George Gershwin congratulated his colleagues on their success. If he was disappointed about being left out, he kept his feelings to himself. It was not until 1944, when Richard Rodgers shared the Pulitzer Prize for *Oklahoma!* with lyricist Oscar Hammerstein II, that the judges recognized a show's composer.

Some of the 450,000 people who went to see *Of Thee I Sing* saw George Gershwin in a new role: orchestra conductor. Gershwin threw himself into the task, using his entire body to lead the symphony. Not only did he conduct with his baton or cigar, but he also signaled to the musicians by shrugging, jutting out a hip, or flashing his eyes. He could not help singing along with his music, and there were moments when his thin, high-pitched voice rattled the actors on stage. George S. Kaufman muttered that the playbill should list Gershwin as a member of the cast.

In early 1932, his work on *Of Thee I Sing* finished, Gershwin took off for a vacation in Havana, Cuba. Even on vacation, Gershwin's life was a mad dash from one activity to the next. He played constant games of golf and made many trips to the racetrack. He wrote to a friend, "I spent two hysterical weeks in Havana, where no sleep was had, but the quantity and quality of fun made up for that."

Of course, part of the fun for Gershwin was hearing Cuban music, which reflects its Spanish and African influences. He listened to musicians play as he sat in an iron chair near a bandstand on the waterfront or sipped crushed pineapple with water and sugar at a sidewalk cafe. He danced with the cafe patrons to rumbas, which are songs with a strong African beat.

Gershwin came home from his vacation to find his father seriously ill. Morris Gershwin had leukemia, which was always fatal in the 1930s. The old man kept his sense of humor and relaxed manner to the end. Frances Gershwin recalled her parents' last visit in the hospital, on May 14, 1932. Morris Gershwin lifted his oxygen mask to inquire, "Well, Rose, when you marry again, will you marry a tall man?" (Rose Gershwin had often wished her husband were taller.) An hour later, Morris Gershwin died.

The sunny music of Havana, playing in George Gershwin's mind in the weeks following his father's death, helped to ease his sorrow. As warming temperatures coaxed flowers to bloom in New York City's parks, he hunted down the instruments that made Cuban music so flashy and exciting. He picked up bongo drums, rhythm sticks, and maracas, which are rattles made from hollow gourds or wood. Like the French taxi horns, the Cuban instruments found their way into a Gershwin composition. This work, titled *Cuban Overture*, delighted in Cuban rhythms. It had its premiere in August at Manhattan's Lewisohn Stadium as part of an all-Gershwin concert. Four musicians playing Cuban instruments stood in front of the orchestra, where the audience had a clear view of them. The program also included *An American in Paris*, the two rhapsodies, and songs from Gershwin's Broadway shows. The 18,000 concert tickets were quickly sold as people thronged the football stadium to hear Gershwin's music and see the composer himself. Thousands of fans had to be turned away. The concert was the first of many all-Gershwin programs presented at Lewisohn Stadium and elsewhere.

Ever since 1924, when Ferde Grofé orchestrated the *Rhapsody in Blue*, a small band of detractors had claimed that other musicians had secretly orchestrated—or perhaps composed—all of Gershwin's serious works. Gershwin now heard a more ominous reproach, that he was part of a "Jewish menace," as anti-Semites warned that Jews were as dangerous to the purity of American music as was African-American jazz. Such statements echoed slogans heard often now in Germany from members of the brown-shirted Nazi party, who preached racism and hatred of Jews. The party's leading figure, Adolf Hitler, who was appointed chancellor of Germany in 1933, blamed the worldwide economic depression on a Jewish-communist plot.

The events in Europe inspired George S. Kaufman and Morrie Ryskind to create a third political comedy, *Let 'Em Eat Cake*. The Gershwins again wrote the score. "If *Strike Up the Band* was a satire on War, and *Of Thee I Sing* one on Politics, *Let 'Em Eat Cake* was a satire on Practically Everything," Ira Gershwin observed. "It trampled on the Extreme Right one moment, the Extreme Left the next."

The show revisits the characters from *Of Thee I Sing* four years later, after President Wintergreen has been voted out of office. With his wife, Mary, and his vice president, Throttlebottom, Wintergreen starts a clothing business, manufacturing blue shirts. He leads an army of blue-shirted soldiers to Washington, D.C., to overthrow the government.

The problem was that no one laughed at the idea of fascism and dictatorship coming to America. And the characters perplexed people. Wintergreen had been the hero of *Of Thee I Sing*. Was he now supposed to be a villain?

Too much of the show was off-target. Even George Gershwin's music rubbed people the wrong way. Gershwin had composed most of the show's songs in counterpoint—that is, with two or more melodies being played or sung at once. The effect was jarring. He told a reporter that the counterpoint "gives my music the acid touch it has." George S. Kaufman quipped, "It's giving me acid indigestion."

Also, Kaufman and Ryskind's satire no longer suited the times. Americans were less cynical than at the start of the depression. They had a new president, Franklin Delano Roosevelt. Under his leadership, Congress had passed laws that gave people jobs, aided farmers, guaranteed workers' rights, and insured bank deposits. The public had new reasons to hope. *Let 'Em Eat Cake* opened in New York in October 1933 and played for only forty-six performances.

A reviewer dismissed the musical, saying, "Sequels are not equals," but George Gershwin was far from discouraged. He was looking ahead, preparing to take on the greatest musical challenge of his life.

Chapter Seven

Spirituals and Folk Songs

One night in 1926, George Gershwin climbed into bed and picked up a book, planning to read himself to sleep. The book, a novel entitled *Porgy*, was a gift from Emily and Lou Paley. Instead of dozing off, though, Gershwin stayed awake all night and read every word. The next day he showed the book to friends and colleagues, saying, "Some day I'll make an opera out of it."

He wrote to the author of *Porgy*, DuBose Heyward, to say the same thing. He warned Heyward that he would need several years of study to prepare for the task. "What I don't know about music is enough to keep me occupied for the rest of a normally long life," he said. He was constantly learning, and he applied his growing knowledge of music to his work.

Porgy, the slender book that captured Gershwin's imagination, describes, love, death, and survival in Catfish Row, a fictional neighborhood of poor African Americans on the Charleston, South Carolina, waterfront. The characters are Gullah people, descendants of enslaved

West Africans who toiled on the marshy Sea Islands, along the Carolina coast. In that isolated setting, the Gullah preserved customs, legends, and beliefs carried to the New World by their ancestors. Their speech is a blend of English and African languages.

DuBose Heyward was a white man, a native of Charleston who had worked alongside African-American stevedores and fishermen in his youth. He saw that the Gullah way of life was dying out as the people came in contact with whites and with African Americans from the North. In his book, he painted a word portrait of the people he knew. He based his main character, Porgy, on a real Charleston beggar, Sammy Smalls. Like Smalls, Porgy is disabled and travels from place to place in a goat cart.

The novel begins on a Saturday night when the men of Catfish Row come together to gamble. A fight breaks out during one of their games and someone is killed. The murderer, a man named Crown, runs off, leaving his girlfriend, Bess, with nowhere to go. Porgy takes her in, and his love for Bess gives her the strength she needs to turn away from Crown's abuse.

The happiness that Bess enjoys with Porgy is short-lived, however. When Crown returns for her in the blackness of night, Porgy stabs the murderer to protect the woman he loves. The police take Porgy away, and Bess falters. Believing that he will be in jail for many years, she takes off for Savannah, Georgia, with a drug dealer called Sportin' Life. But Porgy is merely questioned by the police and released. He returns to Catfish Row at the novel's end, resigned to living out a lonely life.

Heyward set his story in 1912, the year a ruinous hurricane struck Charleston. His characters endure the storm's winds and flooding as they worry about fishermen out on the rough sea. The people care for the storm's orphans; they chant as they bury their dead. Gershwin wanted to bring all of those scenes to life in music.

Opera traditionally had been a European art form. Because most operas were performed in Italian, German, or some other foreign language, Americans considered them entertainment for the elite. Gershwin planned to change all that, to develop "something in American music that would appeal to the many rather than to the cultured few." He wanted to create "opera for the theatre, with drama, humor, song and dance." And no story, he said, was better suited to the project he had in mind than *Porgy*: "First of all, it is American, and I believe that American music should be based on American material."

Gershwin prepared to write his opera while he scored *Strike Up the Band*, *Girl Crazy*, and *Of Thee I Sing. Porgy* was on his mind while he composed *An American in Paris* and the *Second Rhapsody*. He wrote to DuBose Heyward again in 1932 to say that he was ready to start the opera. But more projects came along, and he pushed back the starting date.

Meanwhile, Heyward was growing impatient. Al Jolson had approached him with a plan to turn *Porgy* into a

Broadway musical in which Jolson would play the lead role himself, in blackface. Heyward was short of money during the depression and eager to earn a profit from a musical version of his book, but Gershwin urged him to sit tight. "The sort of thing I should have in mind for PORGY is a much more serious thing than Jolson could ever do," he counseled. Gershwin's opera would be no blackface parody. African Americans were going to sing the roles. It was not until February 1934, after *Let 'Em Eat Cake* had folded, that Heyward heard some welcome news from New York. "I have begun composing music for the First Act," Gershwin stated in a letter.

George Gershwin composed nothing else while he labored on his opera. To earn money, he hosted a radio program, "Music by Gershwin." He played the piano on the air, interviewed guests, and talked about his favorite subject—his music. At times, he played tunes by unknown composers, including his brother Arthur, a stockbroker who wrote songs in his spare time. "Music by Gershwin" was sponsored by Feen-A-Mint, a laxative. Gershwin liked to joke that without Feen-A-Mint, he would have been unable to write *Porgy and Bess*.

Gershwin was now living in a larger and even more lavish home. The fourteen-room, two-story apartment held three pianos. It contained a desk that the composer had designed for himself with a tilted top that was roomy enough for large sheets of music. The desk's many drawers, cubbyholes, and storage bins made it look like

DuBose Heyward's novel *Porgy* inspired George Gershwin to compose an "American opera."

a honeycomb. A direct telephone line connected George's workroom with Ira's new apartment across the street.

While Gershwin worked on the music for his opera, DuBose Heyward started on the libretto. The two men carried on a long-distance collaboration, because Gershwin had to stay in New York to broadcast his radio program, and Heyward worked best in the warm climate and relaxed atmosphere of South Carolina.

Gershwin soon realized he needed a seasoned lyricist at his side. There were times when Heyward's lyrics needed some fixing to match the tune he had devised for them. And Heyward, who had never written songs before, came up with some verses that were cumbersome to sing. It was time for Ira to join the creative team.

In the partnership of George Gershwin, Ira Gershwin, and DuBose Heyward there was none of the fighting that Gershwin had witnessed years earlier when Jerome Kern and Victor Herbert worked on *Miss 1917*. Each of the three men respected the others' skill. No one tried to prove that he was the smartest or most talented. They all cooperated to write the best opera they could.

Still, George Gershwin needed to visit South Carolina, to meet the people of the Sea Islands and hear their music. He took a break from radio when summer came and traveled south with his cousin, the artist Henry Botkin. Gershwin and Botkin spent five weeks in a cabin on Folly Island, ten miles off the coast.

The two city dwellers felt as if they had reached the

edge of the universe. "Imagine, there's not one telephone on the whole Island—public or private," Gershwin wrote to his mother soon after he arrived. Drinking water had to be carried in from the mainland. "Yesterday was the first hot day and it brought out the flies and gnats and mosquitoes," Gershwin wrote. "There are so many swamps in the district that when the breeze comes in from the land there's nothing to do but scratch." Those swamps sheltered alligators that bellowed during the night, making the New Yorkers uneasy in their beds.

"Many, many eerie sand crabs looking very much like glass spiders, crawled around the cottage," Henry Botkin said. "Droves of bugs and insects [flew] against the screen and the noisy crickets drove George to distraction, keeping him awake nights." Convinced that the crickets nested in a certain tree, Gershwin climbed a ladder into its branches, hoping to remove the noisy pests. But crickets were everywhere on Folly Island. There was no way to get rid of them.

In the city, Gershwin had slept until noon, dressed in expensive suits, and smoothed his hair in place. On Folly Island, he was up at 7:30 a.m. to walk or drive on the beach. He wrote music in the morning and worked on lyrics with Heyward in the afternoon. He let his heavy beard grow and left his hair uncombed. He spent the day in swimming trunks, although shark warnings kept him out of the ocean.

"I've never lived in such a back-to-nature place," he

said to Ashley Cooper of the *Charleston News and Courier*, who had come to interview him. He remarked on the fascinating sight of sea turtles coming ashore to lay their eggs on Folly Island's beaches. Earlier, he had written to a friend, "There is music in the turtles, in the rhythm of the laying of their eggs, first one, then two, then one and two eggs at a time."

Gershwin and the reporter spoke for a short time about nature before the subject turned to music. "He couldn't talk about music very long without wanting to play a piano," Ashley Cooper wrote. They went inside the cabin, where Gershwin sat down at an upright piano. "Here's a good one," he said, and launched into "I Got Rhythm." He played one hit after another, as if he were at a New York party. "Although I have always had a voice which has been known to frighten crows, I joined in," Cooper said.

Gershwin played past nightfall. Cooper was surprised when he finally left to see thirty or forty Folly Islanders sitting outside, listening to the music. "Don't know who that man is playing the piano," one of them said. "But that man really can play!"

DuBose Heyward brought Gershwin to neighboring James Island, which had a large Gullah population. There, the composer met the Gullah people in their homes, general stores, one-room schools, and churches. He listened closely to their traditional music, to their folk songs and spirituals, letting the tempos and feelings of the music sink into his memory.

One night, Heyward took his visitor to a Gullah religious service near his home on the mainland. Song-like prayers flowed from the bungalow where the meeting was held. Outside the door, Gershwin held Heyward's arm and whispered to him to listen. Heyward had often heard his neighbors praying, but now he felt as if he were hearing them through Gershwin's ears. As if for the first time, he heard a dozen or so voices mixed in loud prayer. The vocals were sung in rounds, each person beginning at a different time and singing a different theme. Together the singers united into one exciting harmony whose pounding rhythm, Heyward said, was terrifying and intense.

His head filled with music, Gershwin returned to New York and buckled down to work. Unlike musical comedy, the opera would have no spoken scenes, so he would have to create music that set the mood throughout the piece. And then there was the daunting job of orchestrating the opera, which took more than six months.

It was solitary work, and Gershwin hated to spend so much time alone. He often called up Mabel Schirmer, the friend who had helped him find taxi horns in Paris, and invited her to lunch. Schirmer, who was living in New York at this time, spent many afternoons with Gershwin, doing needlework while he labored over his sheets of music. When he finished working each afternoon, he and Mabel took a brisk walk in Central Park.

Gershwin took a break from his work at the end of

December to go to Washington, D.C., to have dinner with President Roosevelt. Being a guest in the White House was a thrilling experience for Gershwin, one that caused him to reflect on his immigrant roots. Kay Halle, his date for the evening, remembered him standing beneath a chandelier in the White House foyer and saying, "If only my father could see me now!"

After dinner, the president had a piano rolled into the East Room and asked Gershwin to play. "With stars in his eyes, and a salute in the direction of the president, George sat down and played 'Wintergreen for President' from his musical *Of Thee I Sing*, with all the guests joining in song," Kay Halle said. Years earlier, polio had left Roosevelt unable to use his legs. Now, Halle observed, "Though the president's legs were in steel braces, he managed to move them ever so slightly in rhythm with the cascade of tunes that poured from George's fingers."

Nine months later, on September 2, 1935, Gershwin sat at his desk and put the final note on the final page of music. The opera was complete. DuBose Heyward gave it the title *Porgy and Bess*.

It was time for the opera to take shape on stage, and Gershwin hovered over the rehearsals like an anxious father with a newborn baby. He auditioned singers and sat in on practice sessions, munching peanuts. Drawing on his research in South Carolina, he taught the performers how to make their characters sound authentic. Many in the African-American cast had been born and educated in the North, and had never even been to the South.

Porgy and Bess was first performed in Boston, on September 30, 1935. Once more, George Gershwin brought something unique to the American theater.

The opera began with a boisterous fanfare. Anyone familiar with the *Rhapsody in Blue* soon recognized the rhythm of a train. Then, the orchestra grew quieter, the beat slowed, and a jazz piano took over. The music carried the audience to a different locale, far from the city's clamor, where time moved at a slumberous pace.

On stage, a woman was rocking her child to sleep, singing a mournful lullaby that sounded like a spiritual. That lullaby was "Summertime," a song that is now known throughout the world.

Gershwin filled *Porgy and Bess* with sounds inspired by the Gullah culture. For example, he recreated the prayer meeting in the music for the opera's hurricane scene. The people of Catfish Row are frightened for their lives as they wait out the storm together. One woman offers up a prayer in song, asking Jesus for protection. At the same time, a man sings to God, beseeching Him to raise His fallen children. A second woman then lifts her voice to call out for mercy. Soon, six people are crying to Heaven at once, each chanting different words, each singing a different tune. The six strands of music twine together and rise heavenward. In this scene, Gershwin showed that even in a crowd, people feel alone in their fear. Each person talks to God in his or her own way.

The songs, or arias, of *Porgy and Bess* flesh out the characters singing them. Porgy sings "I Got Plenty o' Nuthin'," revealing that he is a simple man with few needs. The drug dealer, Sportin' Life, shows himself to be a corrupting influence when he calls on the religious people of Catfish Row to question their beliefs. Gershwin created a slithering, snaking melody for Sportin' Life's aria, causing listeners to compare the drug dealer to the serpent that lived in the Garden of Eden. Yet Gershwin made Sportin' Life appealing and fun. Twice, the dope peddler interrupts his sermon to sing scat, or nonsense words in a jazz style. Gershwin called Sportin' Life "a humorous, dancing villain, who is likable and believable and at the same time evil."

In the opera, Sportin' Life lures Bess to New York while Porgy is away, rather than to Savannah, as he did in Heyward's novel. Unwilling to live in Catfish Row without his woman, Porgy sets out for New York to find her, although he has no clear idea how to get there.

The Boston audiences loved Gershwin's opera. Following one performance, they gave him a standing ovation that lasted fifteen minutes. But *Porgy and Bess* was three hours long—too long for most people to sit through without getting bored, the show's producers feared. Gershwin went to work on the score and cut away nearly a quarter of the music, including the jazz piano in the introduction and the six concurrent prayers. It was painful to toss away so much beautiful music, but a long running

Porgy and Bess is set in Catfish Row, a fictional neighborhood of Charleston, South Carolina.

time could be fatal to a show in New York.

Even with the cuts, New York gave the opera a mixed reception. The critics were still trying to find the right category for Gershwin's music. It was too playful and original to be called classical, yet it was more ambitious than most popular fare. As for *Porgy and Bess*, the critics called it "a hybrid," and "an aggrandized musical show." They complained that it contained show tunes rather than arias.

Gershwin found such fussing about categories tiresome. "Good music is good music, even if you call it 'oysters,' " he said. He defended his creation, stating, "It is true that I have written songs for *Porgy and Bess*. I am not ashamed of writing songs at any time so long as they are good songs. In *Porgy and Bess* I realized I was writing an opera for the theatre and without songs it could be neither of the theatre nor entertaining." He pointed out that many of the arias of European opera were hit songs in their day.

George Gershwin called *Porgy and Bess* a "folk opera." He explained that "Its people naturally would sing folk music." In writing the opera, he had decided not to use authentic folk melodies, because he wanted the piece to have the unified sound of a single composer's work. "I wrote my own spirituals and folksongs," he said.

Financially, *Porgy and Bess* was a failure, barely earning back the money spent to produce it. The critics' opinions kept people away, and with many seats in the theater empty every night, the folk opera closed.

Chapter Eight

Final Years

George Gershwin had brushed off bad reviews in the past, but it was more difficult to do so this time. He had spent nearly two years composing *Porgy and Bess*, and although he still believed it to be an important work, the critics' reactions hurt him deeply. He hoped that a vacation in Mexico would cheer him up.

At art museums and galleries, Gershwin marveled at the way Mexican painters captured the color and spirit of their country. He met some of Mexico's best-known artists, including Diego Rivera, who painted bold murals based on historical and social themes. Another Mexican artist, David Sisqueiros, painted Gershwin in an imaginary scene, sitting at a piano in a concert hall as his friends and relatives fill the first two rows of seats.

Gershwin returned from Mexico feeling only a little bit better than when he left home. But at least a familiar question was on his lips: What will I do next? What came next for George Gershwin was another trip to Hollywood. In 1936, most of Broadway's songwriters were dividing their time between New York and California. They could not count on earning a living from the theater during the depression, and the motion-picture companies paid them highly to write songs for movie musicals.

George, Ira, and Leonore Gershwin flew to California in November 1936. A group of friends came to see the trio off, but one face was missing from the crowd. It belonged to Kay Swift, a pianist and composer.

Gershwin had been spending a great deal of time with Swift, who was divorced and had three daughters, and the relationship had grown serious. Kay wanted to get married, but George could not make up his mind. Finally, they had agreed to spend a year apart, exchanging no letters or telephone calls. They would examine their feelings again when the year was up. Gershwin was now thirty-eight. His reluctance to marry had troubled him. He had consulted a psychiatrist for a while in an attempt to understand his feelings.

The Gershwin brothers worked on the scores for three movies in 1936 and 1937. Two of them starred George's old friend Fred Astaire. Adele Astaire had left show business, so Fred danced with other women in films. He is best remembered for his partnership with Ginger Rogers. Fred Astaire and Ginger Rogers appeared in ten films together in the 1930s and 1940s. The Gershwins scored their seventh film, *Shall We Dance*. They also wrote the songs for *A Damsel in Distress*, featuring Astaire and the husband-and-wife comedy team of George Burns and Gracie Allen.

George Gershwin wrote the music for the 1937 film *Shall We Dance*, starring Fred Astaire and Ginger Rogers.

Creating *Porgy and Bess* had refined the brothers' songwriting skills, and they wrote some of their most enduring songs on this trip to Hollywood. They grew closer than ever, even living in the same house, a mansion in Beverly Hills with a swimming pool, tennis courts, and palm trees shading the driveway.

Everyday speech still appealed to Ira. Now he noticed that Americans pronounced certain words in different ways. That observation resulted in the lyrics to "Let's Call the Whole Thing Off," from *Shall We Dance*, a song in which two lovers consider ending their romance because their ways of speaking keep them apart.

George Gershwin was constantly on the go in Hollywood. When he wasn't composing, he was playing golf or tennis. He walked six miles a day in the Hollywood hills, and he attended parties with movie stars at night. He painted portraits of Jerome Kern and his new friend and tennis partner, Arnold Schoenberg. Schoenberg was one of the most significant composers of the twentieth century. He had fled his native Austria when Hitler came to power in Germany, and he now taught at the University of Southern California. Gershwin provided scholarships for students wanting to study with Schoenberg.

All in all, Hollywood was fun, Gershwin wrote to Mabel Schirmer, although he admitted that "there are depressing moments, too, when talk of Hitler and his gang creep[s] into the conversation." He went on to say, "Ira, of course, loves it out here. He can relax much more than in the East—and you know how Ira loves his relaxation."

While in California, Gershwin flew across the West and Midwest to give concerts. He visited Seattle, Detroit, St. Louis, and other cities. The concert series wound up in February 1937, with two performances near his home base, in Los Angeles, California.

People who knew Gershwin well noticed a change in him during these concerts. The electrifying composer who had always played his music flawlessly now slipped up more often. Pianist Oscar Levant suspected that something was wrong during the first concert in Los Angeles when Gershwin and the orchestra played the *Concerto in F*. "Though he had played the 'Concerto' dozens of times in public with great fluency I noticed that he stumbled on a very easy passage in the first movement," Levant wrote. Later in the piece, Gershwin's fingers tripped again.

While conducting the orchestra the next night, Gershwin caught a whiff of burning rubber, yet no one else smelled anything strange. Suddenly, his head began to ache so severely that it made him dizzy. But he felt better after a short rest and pronounced himself healthy and fit. His friends sighed in relief.

In May, as soon as the score for *A Damsel in Distress* was ready, George and Ira started to work on a third motion picture, *The Goldwyn Follies*, which was to be a costly production with sparkling costumes, spectacular dance routines, and an all-star cast. Now, George admitted to being tired, something he never had complained about before, and he was having more headaches and dizzy spells. He wished Goldwyn's studio had given him a vacation between films. He was weary of the glitter, and he wrote to Mabel Schirmer, "There's nothing like the phony glamour of Hollywood to bring out the need for one's real friends."

George Gershwin had never learned how to slow down, though. In spite of his fatigue and his busy schedule, he planned projects for the coming years. He thought about composing a symphony or a piece for string instruments. He was tempted to start another opera, and Broadway beckoned as well. He imagined a musical comedy about American history in which Rip Van Winkle, the fictional character who slept for twenty years, wakes up in various eras to witness historic events. Gershwin asked himself, how would it be to set the Gettysburg Address to music? And he told his cousin Henry Botkin, "Henry, this year I've got to get married."

Then the headaches came back and grew worse than ever, and work became impossible. Outside a Hollywood restaurant, Gershwin fell to the sidewalk in pain. He sat on the curb holding his head in his hands. Light hurt his eyes, so he spent much of the day indoors with the window shades pulled down. He tried everything he could think of to ease the torment, but nothing worked. In desperation, he took to wearing a mechanical device that fit over the head and was meant to make hair grow. He thought the machine just might make him feel better.

Of course, it didn't. He started losing his temper, which he had never done before.

Ira and Leonore were worried. They insisted that George get medical help, but a doctor examined him and found nothing wrong. To be sure that something had not been missed, George entered a hospital for tests on June 23. There, physicians x-rayed his head and checked his eyes, lungs, and nervous system but found no sign of illness.

Gershwin's friends discussed his condition and decided that it was caused by nerves, like his composer's stomach. The friends took a firm approach with him, urging him to ignore his symptoms and get on with his life. They thought that any show of sympathy would only encourage him to remain ill. By now, Gershwin slept most of the time. When he was awake, he stumbled on the stairs and dropped forks and pencils. He had trouble feeding himself. Nothing anyone said or did made any difference.

S. N. Behrman visited him in early July and was shocked at his old friend's pale, sickly appearance. "The light had gone from his eyes," Behrman observed. "He seemed old. He greeted me mirthlessly. His handshake was limp, the spring had gone out of his walk."

Behrman was most alarmed at Gershwin's refusal to play the piano. The George Gershwin he had always known would never have passed up a chance to play. Behrman understood that he was not looking at someone with a psychological problem. Gershwin was physically ill, and his condition was grave. "I had a sinking feeling: he is no longer with us," Behrman said.

On Friday, July 9, Gershwin slipped into a coma. The doctors at Cedars of Lebanon Hospital suspected he had a brain tumor, although nothing abnormal showed up on their x-rays. A brain operation offered the only possibility of saving his life.

George's family and physicians wanted the best possible doctor to perform the surgery. They sent for the top neurosurgeon in the country, Dr. Walter Dandy of the Johns Hopkins Medical School, in Baltimore, Maryland. It turned out that Dandy was spending the weekend aboard a yacht in the middle of Chesapeake Bay, far from any telephones. Friends of the Gershwin family appealed to President Roosevelt for help. After Maryland State Police contacted the yacht by short-wave radio, the White House authorized the Coast Guard to pick Dandy up. It was now Saturday, July 10.

While all that was happening, the doctors in California located another fine neurosurgeon, Dr. Howard Naffziger. Naffziger interrupted his vacation in Nevada to fly to Los Angeles and examine George Gershwin. In Naffziger's opinion, the surgery had to be done right away. He conferred by telephone with Dr. Dandy on the East Coast, and then made arrangements for the operation, which he would perform. The procedure was to begin after midnight, in the first hours of Sunday, July 11.

Mourners crowded Fifth Avenue on July 15, 1937, to attend the funeral of George Gershwin.

The delicate surgery lasted five hours. Dr. Naffziger probed deep within George's brain, where he discovered a glioblastoma, a deadly form of tumor that was large and impossible to treat. The surgeon knew that he could do nothing to help this patient.

Orderlies wheeled Gershwin back to his hospital room at seven in the morning. And a little while later, he was gone. George Gershwin died at 10:35 a.m., with Ira at his bedside. He was thirty-eight years old.

Rain hushed New York City on July 15, 1937, the day George Gershwin was buried. Temple Emanu-El on Fifth Avenue was filled to capacity for the funeral. Hundreds had been turned away at the door. More than a thousand mourning fans stood behind police barricades on both sides of the avenue, paying their last respects. From where they stood, they heard the familiar notes of the *Rhapsody in Blue*. They watched a slow procession of honorary pall bearers—past and present mayors of the city, performers, composers, and conductors—escort Gershwin's casket from the synagogue.

The religious service ended and the crowd dispersed, but feelings of sadness and disbelief lingered. Todd Duncan, Gershwin's first Porgy, watched Al Jolson walk along the white line in the middle of Fifth Avenue, oblivious to the cars hurrying past on both sides.

For Ira Gershwin, the loss of his brother was devastating. He did almost no work at all for three years. At last, his grief let up enough for him to write the lyrics for *Lady in the Dark*, a show with music by the German composer Kurt Weill. Ira continued to work as a Broadway and Hollywood lyricist until 1954. He helped choose the music for *An American in Paris*, a film released in 1951 that featured George Gershwin's tone poem and a number of Gershwin songs.

Gershwin's music continues to be heard. Musicians regularly perform his orchestral works and songs. *Porgy and Bess* lives on as well. In the 1950s, American performers presented a shortened version of the opera in Central and South America, the Middle East, and Europe. It became the first American opera to be performed at La Scala, Italy's foremost opera house.

In 1976, the Houston Grand Opera restored the sections that had been cut from *Porgy and Bess*. The world at last discovered Gershwin's masterpiece in its fullness, as the composer had intended it to be heard. The restored *Porgy and Bess* is the version usually performed today.

Many people have wondered what George Gershwin would have accomplished if he had lived longer. A radio interviewer once asked Kay Swift to speculate on what Gershwin might have done. She said, "We'll never know, will we? But it would have been important." We can only imagine the soaring, spirited music that would have continued to flow from his nimble mind and fingers.

Major Works

1919—La, La, Lucille
1924—Rhapsody in Blue
—Lady, Be Good
—Primrose
—Sweet Little Devil
1925—Tip-Toes
—Oh, Kay!
—Concerto in F
1927—Funny Face
—Strike Up the Band (first version)
—Three Piano Preludes
1928—An American in Paris
1929—Strike Up the Band (second version)
1930—Girl Crazy
1931—Second Rhapsody
—Of Thee I Sing
—Delicious
1932—Cuban Overture
1933—Let 'Em Eat Cake
1934—Variations on "I Got Rythym"
1935—Porgy and Bess
1937—A Damsel in Distress
—Shall We Dance
1945—Rhapsody in Blue (motion picture)
1951—An American in Paris (motion picture)

Glossary
of Musical Terms

aria: A composition for solo voice with musical accompaniment.

concerto: A piece of music written for both orchestra and soloist (or small group). The concerto usually moves through three sections that alternate in tempo (fast, slow, fast), and emphasizes the contrast between soloist and orchestra.

crescendo: An increase in loudness. *Diminuendo* indicates a decrease in loudness.

glissando: The playing of rapid scales using a sliding movement.

libretto: The text of an opera.

meter: The pattern of fixed beats in a piece of music.

pentatonic scale: A scale that has five notes per octave, most notably occuring in non-Western music.

prelude: A piece of music that introduces a longer work. Beginning in the nineteenth century, however, the term *prelude* also referred to a short, independent musical work.

rhapsody: The term used liberally to describe a piece of music that suggests grandiosity or fantasy and that may be nationalistic and heroic.

syncopation: A momentary change in the prevailing meter in a piece of music. Syncopation is a diversifying technique that has been used for centuries, but is best known to the twentieth century in ragtime music.

tone poem: An orchestral work that portrays a story, scene, poem, or other nonmusical idea.

Bibliography

Alpert, Hollis. *The Life and Times of Porgy and Bess: The Story of an American Classic.* New York: Alfred A. Knopf, 1990.

Armitage, Merle, ed. *George Gershwin.* New York: Longmans, Green and Company, 1938.

Astaire, Fred. *Steps in Time.* New York: Harper and Row, 1959.

Behrman, S. N. *People in a Diary: A Memoir.* Boston: Little, Brown and Company. 1972.

_____. "Troubadour." *New Yorker,* May 25, 1929, pp. 27-29.

Blockson, Charles L. "Sea Change in the Sea Islands: 'Nowhere to Lay Down Weary Head.' " *National Geographic,* December 1987, pp. 735-763.

Collier, James Lincoln. *Inside Jazz.* New York: Four Winds Press, 1973.

Cooper, John Milton, Jr. *Pivotal Decades: The United States, 1900-1920.* New York: W. W. Norton and Company, 1990.

Creel, Margaret Washington. *"A Peculiar People": Slave Religion and Community-Culture among the Gullahs.* New York: New York University Press, 1988.

Ewen, David. *David Ewen Introduces Modern Music.* Philadelphia: Chilton Book Company, 1969.

The George and Ira Gershwin Song Book. New York: Simon and Schuster, 1960.

Gershwin, George. *George Gershwin's Song Book.* New York: Simon and Schuster, 1932.

_____. "Rhapsody in Catfish Row." *New York Times,* October 20, 1935, sec. 10, pp. 1-2.

Gershwin, Ira. *Lyrics on Several Occasions.* New York: Alfred A. Knopf, 1959.

_____. "Which Came First?" *Saturday Review,* August 29, 1959, pp. 31-33, 45.

Goldberg, Isaac. *George Gershwin: A Study in American Music.* New York: Frederick Ungar, 1931.

_____. *Tin Pan Alley.* New York: The John Day Company, 1930.

Halle, Kay. "The Time of His Life." *Washington Post,* February 5, 1978, sec. F, pp. 1, 5.

Green, Harvey. *The Uncertainty of Everyday Life: 1915-1945.* New York: HarperCollins, 1992.

Heyward, DuBose. *Porgy.* New York: George H. Doran Company, 1926.

Howe, Irving and Kenneth Libo. *How We Lived: A Documentary History of Immigrant Jews in America, 1880-1930.* New York: Rich ard Marek Publishers, 1979.

Jablonski, Edward. *Gershwin: A Biography.* New York: Doubleday, 1987.

_____. *Gershwin Remembered.* Portland, OR: Amadeus Press, 1992.

Kendall, Alan. *George Gershwin.* New York: Universe Books, 1987.

Kimball, Robert and Alfred Simon. *The Gershwins.* New York: Atheneum, 1973.

Levant, Oscar. *A Smattering of Ignorance.* Garden City, NY: Doubleday and Company, 1959.

Meredith, Scott. *George S. Kaufman and His Friends.* Garden City, NY: Doubleday and Company, 1974.

Perrett, Geoffrey. *America in the Twenties: A History.* New York: Simon and Schuster, 1982.

Politoske, Daniel T. *Music.* Englewood Cliffs, NJ: Prentice-Hall, 1988.

Rockwell, John. "The Genius of Gershwin Still Inspires Composers." *New York Times,* March 8, 1987, pp. 23, 36.

Rosenberg, Deena. *Fascinating Rhythm: The Collaboration of George and Ira Gershwin.* New York: Dutton, 1991.

Schlesinger, Arthur M., Jr. "How History Upstaged the Gershwins." *New York Times,* April 5, 1987, p. 7.

Schoener, Allon. *Portal to America: The Lower East Side, 1870-1925.* New York: Holt, Rinehart and Winston, 1967.

Taubman, Howard. *The Making of the American Theatre.* New York: Coward McCann, Inc., 1967.

Sources

CHAPTER ONE

p. 10, "I remember being..." Gershwin, Ira. *The George and Ira Gershwin Song Book*. New York: Simon and Schuster, 1960, p. vi.

p. 10, "The peculiar jumps..." Goldberg, Isaac. *George Gershwin: A Study in American Music*. New York: Frederick Ungar, 1931, p. 54.

p. 11, "...standing there barefoot..." Ibid.

p. 11, "...flashing revelation of beauty." Ibid., p. 58.

p. 14, "...very easy-going, humorous..." Jablonski, op. cit., p. 4.

p. 17, "I rubbed my fingers..." Goldberg, op. cit., p. 60.

p. 17, "...and not with an apple on his head, either!" Ibid.

p. 17, "I have a new pupil..." Goldberg, op. cit., p. 61.

CHAPTER TWO

p. 23, "Wouldn't it be great..." Astaire, Fred. *Steps in Time*. New York: Harper and Row, 1959, p. 55.

p. 23, "George took it down...." Rosenberg, op. cit., p. 25.

p. 24, "He handed me five dollars...."Jablonski, op. cit., p. 19.

p. 26, "Who told you..." Ibid., p. 22.

p. 29, "A New Up-to-the-Minute..." Kimball and Simon, op. cit., p. 23.

p. 29, "Whisking his hand across..." Gershwin, Ira. "Which Came First?" *Saturday Review*, August 29, 1959, p. 33.

p. 30, "...now vivacious and surprising..." Jablonski, op. cit., p. 37.

CHAPTER THREE

p. 32, "Two circular staircases..." Kendall, Alan. *George Gershwin*. New York: Universe Books, p. 39.

p. 33, "...love, hate, passion, [and] jealousy." Jablonski, op. cit., p. 51.

p. 34, "The audience was as much fun..." Ibid., p. 59.

p. 35, "...ended by surrendering completely..." Ibid.

p. 35, "Even then her hearers..." Ibid., p. 60.

p. 35, "...the age of sophisticated jazz." Ibid.

p. 36, "I heard it as a sort..." Goldberg, op. cit., p. 139.

p. 36, "I wrote it in ten days." Jablonski, op. cit., p. 65.

p. 36, "I don't believe the rhapsody..." Jablonski, op. cit., p. 65.

p. 41, "At half-past five on the afternoon..." Ibid., p. 72 .

p. 41, "If this way lies the path..." Jablonski, op. cit., p. 73.

p. 41, "The Rhapsody hinted at something..." Rosenberg, op. cit., p. 61.

p. 42, "...structural uncertainty..." Ibid.

p. 42, "...melodic and harmonic anemia." Ibid.

p. 42, "...weep over the lifelessness..." Jablonski, op. cit., p. 72.

p. 43, "It remained for George Gershwin..." Rosenberg, op. cit., p. 61.

CHAPTER FOUR

p. 44, "An evening with..." Meredith, Scott. *George S. Kaufman and His Friends.* Garden City, N.Y.: Doubleday and Company, 1974, p. 409.

p. 45, "George, if you had..." Ibid.

p. 45, "Ira's a hard man..." Rosenberg, op. cit., p. 107.

p. 45, "Someone opened the door..." Behrman, S. N. *People in a Diary.* Boston: Little, Brown and Company, 1972, p. 244.

p. 45, "About forty people..." Ibid.

p. 46, "I went to the door," Ibid.

p. 46, "We stopped bothering..." Ibid.

p. 46, "...misplaced accents." Jablonski, op. cit., p. 83.

p. 47, "For God's sake, George," Jablonski, op. cit., p. 83.

p. 47, "It was a tricky rhythm..." Gershwin, Ira. *Lyrics on Several Occasions.* New York: Alfred A. Knopf, 1959, p. 173.

p. 48, "Adele and I..." Astaire, op. cit., p. 134.

p. 48, "For days I couldn't find one." Ibid.

p. 48, "There was a lot going on..." Ibid., p. 135.

p. 49, "Many people thought the *Rhapsody*..." Goldberg, op. cit., p. 205.

p. 49, "...to show them that there was..." Ibid.

p. 50, "George would..." Kimball and Simon, op. cit., p. 50.

p. 51, "Three or four young men..." Behrman, S. N. "Troubadour." *New Yorker*, May 25, 1929, p. 27.

p. 51, "I asked for George, or his brother Ira." Ibid.

p. 51, "No one bothered to reply, " Ibid.

p. 51, "Who under the sun," Ibid.

p. 51, "To tell you the truth...for a game." Ibid.

p. 52, "I am rooting hard..." Kimball and Simon, op. cit., p. 52.

p. 54, "He alone actually expresses us." Jablonski, op. cit., p. 106.

p. 54, "...an instinctive artist..." Ibid.

p. 54, "...conventional, [and] trite..." Ibid.

p. 54, "Here lies the body...Composer? American?" Ibid., p. xiv.

p. 55, "Pursue musical studies..." Rosenberg, op. cit., p. 62.

p. 55, "Further study will..." Ibid.

p. 55, "...agreeable and remunerative." Jablonski, op. cit., p. 88.

CHAPTER FIVE

p. 56, "...a fairly busy young composer..." Jablonski, op. cit., p. 78.

p. 57, "He never made me feel..." Kimball and Simon, op. cit., p. 138.

p. 58, "I would be heartbroken—" Ewen, David. *David Ewen Introduces Modern Music*. Philadelphia: Chilton Book Co., 1969, p. 215.

p. 58, "Don't ever let Ira..." Kimball and Simon, op. cit., p. 80.

p. 61, "Boy how my legs..."Jablonski, op. cit., p. 162.

p. 62, "...to be handled lightly, " Rosenberg, op. cit., p. 164.

p. 62, "The opening gay section..." Ibid.

p. 62, "...the spirit of the music..." Ibid.

p. 63, "...easily the best piece..." Jablonski, op. cit., p. 180.

p. 63, "Nauseous claptrap..." Ibid.

p. 63, "...dull, patchy, thin," Ibid.

p. 64, "George Gershwin is a leader..." Ibid., p. 178.

p. 64, "In the rhythm, the melody..." Ibid., p. 179.

p. 65, "Music is design—melody is line; harmony is color." Ibid., p. 18.

CHAPTER SIX

p. 70, "Nearly everybody comes back..." Goldberg, op. cit., p. 273.

p. 71, "Vote for Prosperity..." Meredith, op. cit., p. 432.

p. 73, "I spent two hysterical weeks..." Jablonski, op. cit., p. 227.

p. 73, "Well, Rose, when you marry again," Ibid.

p. 75, "If *Strike Up the Band*..." Gershwin, Ira. *Lyrics on Several Occasions*, p. 162.

p. 76, "...gives my music the acid touch it has." Meredith, op. cit., p. 462.

p. 76, "It's giving me acid indigestion." Ibid.

p. 76, "Sequels are not equals." Ibid., p. 464.

CHAPTER SEVEN

p. 77, "Some day I'll make an opera out of it." Jablonski, Edward, ed. *Gershwin Remembered*. Portland, Or.: Amadeus Press, 1992, p. 93.

p. 77, "What I don't know..." Ewen, op. cit., p. 216.

p. 79, "...something in American..." Gershwin, George. "Rhapsody in Catfish Row." *New York Times*, October 20, 1935, sec. 10, p. 1.

p. 79, "...opera for the theatre," Ibid., p. 2.

p. 79, "First of all, it is American," Ibid., p. 1.

p. 80, "The sort of thing..." *Gershwin Remembered*, op. cit., p. 96.

p. 80, "I have begun composing music for the First Act." Ibid., p. 97.

p. 82, "Imagine, there's not one..." Alpert, Hollis. *The Life and Times of Porgy and Bess*. New York: Alfred A. Knopf., 1990, p. 88.

p. 83, "Yesterday was the first..." Ibid.

p. 83, "There are so many swamps..." Ibid.

p. 83, "Many, many eerie..." *Gershwin Remembered*, op. cit., p. 101.

p. 83, "Droves of bugs and insects..." Ibid.

p. 83, "I've never lived in such a back-to-nature place." Ibid., p. 102.

p. 84, "There is music in the turtles," Halle, Kay. "The Time of His Life." *Washington Post*, February 5, 1978, sec. F, p. 5.

p. 84, "He couldn't talk about..." *Gershwin Remembered*, op. cit., p. 102.

p. 84, "Here's a good one." Ibid.

p. 84, "Although I have always..." Ibid.

p. 84, "Don't know who.." Ibid.

p. 86, "If only my father could see me now!" Halle, op. cit., p. 5.

p. 86, "With stars in his eyes...joining in song." Ibid.

p. 86, "Though the president's...from George's fingers." Ibid.

p. 88, "...a humorous, dancing villain," Gershwin, George. "Rhapsody in Catfish Row," op. cit., p. 1.

p. 90, "...a hybrid..." Jablonski, op. cit., p. 289.

p. 90, "...an aggrandized musical show." Ibid.

p. 90, "Good music is good..." *Gershwin Remembered*, op. cit., p. 168.

p. 90, "It is..." Gershwin, George. "Rhapsody in Catfish Row," op. cit., p. 1.

p. 90, "Its people naturally would sing folk music." Ibid.

p. 90, "I wrote my own spirituals and folksongs." Ibid.

CHAPTER EIGHT

p. 94, "there are depressing moments," Rosenberg, op. cit., p. 352.

p. 94, "Ira, of course...loves his relaxation." Ibid.

p. 95, "Though he had played the 'Concerto'..." Levant, op. cit., p. 145.

p. 96, "There's nothing like..." Rosenberg, op. cit., p. 353.

p. 96, "Henry, this year..." Kimball and Simon, op. cit., p. 216.

p. 97, "The light had gone..." Behrman, *People in a Diary*, op. cit., p. 253.

p. 98, "I had a sinking feeling..." Jablonski, op. cit., p. 321.

p. 101, "We'll never know, will we..." Jablonski, op. cit., p. 326.

Index

Aarons, Alex, 29, 46
Actor's Dinner Club, 67
Aeolian Hall, 35, 39, 43
"Alexander's Ragtime Band," 20, 34
Allen, Gracie, 92
An American in Paris, (motion picture), 101
An American in Paris, 63, 74
Americana, 67
Arrangement in Black and Grey No. 1, 38
Astaire, Adele, 22, 46-48, 58, 92
Astaire, Fred, 22, 46-48, 58, 92

Bayes, Nora, 28
Beethoven Society Orchestra, 16
Behrman, S. N., 50-51, 97-98
Benton, Thomas Hart, 65
Berlin, Irving, 20, 23, 34, 52
"Blue Monday," 33, 56
Boston Evening Transcript, 30
Botkin, Henry, 64, 82, 96
"Brother, Can You Spare a Dime?", 67
Burns, George, 92

Carnegie Hall, 52
Caesar, Irvng 30-31
Charleston News and Courier, 83
Chatauqua Institute, 49
Chopin, Frederic, 17
Chotzinoff, Samuel, 43, 52, 54
Cohan, George M., 28

Concerto in F, 51, 54, 56, 63, 95
Cooper, Ashley, 83-84
Cuban Overture, 74

Damrosch, Walter, 49, 55
A Damsel in Distress, 92, 95
Dandy, Walter, 98
De Sylva, Buddy, 33, 35, 55
Debussy, Claude, 17
Delicious, 68
Dietz, Howard, 45-46
"Do It Again," 35
Duncan, Todd, 100

An Experiment in Modern Music, 35, 40, 43

"Fascinating Rhythm," 47
Funny Face, 58

Gaugin, Paul, 65
Gauthier, Eva, 34-35
Gershwin, Arthur, 16, 50-51, 64
Gershwin, Frances, 16, 50, 61, 64, 73
Gershwin, George,
    and art, 64-65, 91
    childhood, 9-21
    criticism, 30, 35, 41-43, 52, 54, 63-64, 76, 84, 88, 90-91
    death, 100
    education, 10, 12, 16-17, 21
    in Europe, 46, 61-63

funeral, 100
girlfriends, 57-58, 86, 92
in Hollywood, 68, 92, 94-99, 100
illness, 95-100
performances, 31, 34, 39-41, 51-52, 56, 95
radio show, 80, 82
recreation, 46, 73, 94
as song plugger, 21-25, 28
in South Carolina, 82-85
Gershwin, Ira, 9-10, 14, 16, 25, 28-29, 35, 38, 45-46, 48-52, 56-58, 60-61, 64-67, 72, 75, 82, 92-93, 95, 97, 99, 101
Gershwin, Leonore, 57, 60-61, 64, 92, 97
Gershwin, Morris, 9, 12, 14, 16, 21, 30-31, 50, 73-74
Gershwin, Rose, 9-10, 12, 14, 16, 21, 50, 73
Girl Crazy, 68, 67, 79
The Goldwyn Follies, 95
Gottschalk, Louis Moreau, 42
Grofé, Ferde, 38-39, 74

Halle, Kay, 86
Hambitzer, Charles, 16-17, 21, 28
Hammerstein, Oscar II, 72
Herbert, Victor, 26, 39, 82
Heyward, DuBose, 77-80, 82-88
Hitler, Adolf, 75
Hutcheson, Ernest, 49-50

"I Got Plenty o' Nuthin'," 89
"I Got Rhythm," 67, 84
"I Was So Young (You Were So Beautiful)," 28
"I'll Build a Stairway to Paradise," 32-33

The Jazz Singer, 68
Jerome H. Remick and Company, 21-22, 23
Jolson, Al, 31, 33, 68, 79, 80, 100

Joplin, Scott, 18

Kahn, Otto, 64
Kaufman, George S., 59-61, 66, 70-73, 75-77
Kern, Jerome, 26, 82, 94
Kilenyi, Edward, 17, 55

La, La, Lucille, 29
Ladies First, 28
Lady in the Dark, 100
Lady, Be Good!, 46, 48
Lawrence, Gertrude, 57
Let 'Em Eat Cake, 75-76, 80
"Let's Call the Whole Thing Off," 94
Levant, Oscar, 44, 95
Lewisohn Stadium, 74
"Livery Stable Blues," 39

"Mah-Jongg," 32
Melody in F, 10
Merman, Ethel, 67
Metropolitan Opera, 64
Miss 1917, 26, 32, 82
Music Box Theater, 72

Naffziger, Howard, 98-100
New York Symphony Orchestra, 51
New York World, 34, 43
Nocturne in Black and Gold, 38

Of Thee I Sing, 71-73, 74, 79, 86
Oh, Kay!, 56-57
Oklahoma!, 72
"Over There," 28

Paley, Emily, 45, 57, 77
Paley, Lou, 45, 77
The Passing Show of 1916, 25
Picasso, Pablo, 65
Porgy and Bess, 80, 86-88, 90-91, 94
Porgy, 77-80

Primrose, 46
Pulitzer Prize, 72

Rachmaninoff, Sergei, 39
"Ragging the Traumerei," 21
"The Real American Folk Song (Is a Rag)," 28
Rhapsody in Blue, 38, 40-44, 46, 52, 54, 62, 74, 87, 100
Rivera, Diego, 91
Rodgers, Richard, 72
Rogers, Ginger, 92
Romberg, Sigmund, 25
Roosevelt, Franklin Delano, 76, 86, 98
Rosenzweig, Maxie, 12
Rossini, Gioacchino, 17
Roth, Murray, 24-25
Royale, Selena, 67
Rubenstein, Anton, 12
Ryskind, Morrie, 66, 70-72, 75

"'S Wonderful," 58
Scandals, 32-33
Schirmer, Mabel, 63, 85, 94, 96
Schoenberg, Arnold, 94
Schumann, Robert, 21
Second Rhapsody, 70, 79
Shall We Dance, 92, 94
Sinbad, 31
"Since I Found You," 20
Sisqueiros, David, 91
"Someone to Watch Over Me," 56-57
Song of the Flame, 56
Sousa, John Philip, 39
Stage Relief Fund, 67
Strike Up the Band, 59-60, 66, 75, 79
"Summertime," 87
"Swanee," 31, 44
Sweet Little Devil, 34, 36
Swift, Kay, 92, 101
Swiss Family Robinson, 60

Times Square Theater, 66
Tip-Toes, 56
"Tune into J.O.Y.," 32

Vanity Fair, 54
Vodery, Will, 33
Von Tilzer, Harry, 24

"When You Want 'em You Can't Get 'em, When You Got 'em You Don't Want 'em," 24
Whistler, James McNeill, 38
Whistler's Mother, 38
White, George, 32-34
Whiteman, Paul, 34-36, 39-41, 43, 56
Wilhelm Tell, 17
Wynn, Ed, 25